M000084929

Live, Laugh, Learn

By

Julianne Boling

Live, Laugh and Learn

By: Julianne Roper Boling

I never thought too much about what was stored in the spare room in my brain, especially the one that I have carried with me all my life. The one in my mind where I place all manner of useless junk and ideas I may use later, and many containers of memories.

When I traipse through this spare room, I am amazed at what is hidden in the boxes and crawl spaces. There among the mementoes of the past I can conjure up people, places and events of a lifetime. No matter how often I climb the steps to my mind's "attic", there are always sights and sounds that draw me into the past.

Perhaps, you have not ventured into the spaces of your mind or you don't dare travel back that far. If you experienced a happy childhood, or a sad one, the memories you have retained will show lessons learned and character builders you boxed away at an earlier time.

Much of our world is built around the spaces that we did not think were important at the time. One box holds penny postcards from families on vacation; and carefully held together by a ribbon, are letters and cards from loved ones who were far away. One box holds little stuffed animal, especially the ones needed for your child to fall asleep. In another box are cute little handmade cards and clay sculptures that were treasured by a child and proudly given to you on a special day.

Our life is like a book that we read one page at a time. Some pages are funny and we laugh and others are tragic and we cry. At times we picture ourselves as the heroine but at another time we know for sure we were probably the villains. As we turn the pages of our book there are many chapters that are boring because of the sheer lack of enthusiasm from the main character, our self, and we yawn.

Chapter after chapter there appears to be incidents and situations that are impossible at the beginning but as the plot unfolds, they become necessary in "our book". Circumstances that appear unimportant become integral parts of our story and we have many lessons to learn and pages will be added before we are finished. Many episodes will become adventures but as each event concludes we may understand they did not challenge us, capture our imagination, or add details to the plot and we will discard these chapters as unnecessary.

The further we "read" in our book the more important the characters become. Perhaps we will have only fleeting glimpses of some person from a faraway time and place who did not grow to be an important character in our book. They remain nameless and featureless and their true identity is lost. The secondary characters will appear for brief moments in time, often offering an insight, a solution, a way out or a way through a difficult maze. When we define the main characters in our life story we realize they provide the soul and body of our book.

As our story unfolds we will want to re-read certain chapters that were important, but alas, time is short. We will want to comprehend each line and sentence, identify the people, places, events and encounters, and especially define the remarkable difference a particular character has made to our story. As insight and hindsight come together, we will know that the "author of our book" did not use incidents to punish us but rather to show us our own strengths and weaknesses. We will begin to realize as we move our bookmark further into our lives that so many details are unnecessary, but the timing, while not always our choice or to our liking, is usually appropriate.

Like any good book we hate to reach the final chapter. We dread the outcome, worrying about whether the ending will be to our satisfaction, and as we turn each page we wish for a sequel to the book we have written. Our book can be a best seller or it can be the conclusion of a very poor, unorganized, irrelevant and unimportant work, bound in fancy covers, but not worth the price of the colorful dust jacket.

In my book are characters that are steady and faithful heroes that have made life happy and meaningful. Longtime friendships have survived every adventure and every turn and bump in the road. They have ventured from page to page, chapter to chapter, through many years. Their words are significant and their expressions of concern and caring are "imprinted on many pages". Their faces and identities are underlined and important. These main characters have survived the test of time, the editing and discarding, and have become the heart and soul of my book that I call my attic.

No longer do I stand amazed in my attic because for many years I have shared my treasures with readers of our local newspaper, The Forsyth County News. No longer do I flinch when I realize how old an item has gotten to be in the last year or so. I don't even have to hesitate when I recall the 50's and 60's as wonderful years of growing up and out of my parent's home.

Now I look forward to climbing those stairs of remembrance of events, people and situations. I check out the trunks filled with advice I have collected over the years and recall that at one time or another I hesitated to accept some of these tidbits from my own parents or from my in-laws. Those old clichés and the age-old advice given to me as a child are moth eaten and flimsy from non-use, or over use.

I continue to dust them off and realize there is still a little use left in them. I pass these "gems" along to young mothers, and share them with my own children. Remembering always that each generation has other needs and other instructions to learn, I often box away those same tidbits to be used at another time and place. Hopefully, someone will find my box and these same words will be repeated to the next generation.

If I had my life to live over...

If there is one thing I have learned it is that you cannot live in the past. I need to write something here that says not to let the past keep you from enjoying the present. Dealing with the present and looking expectantly to the future requires all our attention and that seems to be enough.

All of the advice, words of wisdom, and clichés about moving on, life goes on, put it behind you, forgive and forget always seem to spring up and slap me in the face. When I hear this remark, I wonder how the speaker has learned to follow his or her own advice.

Turning loose and letting go of all of the misadventures and mistakes of my past has been a constant and ever demanding aspect of living. Explaining my mistakes to growing boys and convincing them that they should not make those same mistakes is just one example.

We all know our parents were not perfect. Those first television shows about father knowing best and leaving it to Beaver and their perfect households were fictional. These episodes always had happy endings and everyone learned a good lesson, the easy way.

Reality is that the lessons we learned growing up still smack us when we least expect it. The tales of adventures, while humorous and often speak of a more lenient society, also tell of our good fortune in growing up in one piece and without a criminal record.

Why am I writing this and what am I trying to convey? The best I can tell is that I want the reader to realize that going back and going forward require two different attitudes. When the past keeps dredging up unhappiness and ill will the past loses its usefulness. It comes down to moving forward with determination to avoid similar mistakes and miscalculations again.

Erma Bombeck wrote: If I had my life to live over again..." Taking her thoughts, if I had to live my life over again I would probably make the same mistakes. I would probably get punished more often because I would be caught more often doing things I shouldn't. I would probably say many things wrong, and leave undone many things I should do.

However, if I did have my life to live over, I would try to pay more attention to the guidelines and attitudes my parents tried to teach me. I would also forgive the imperfections in others and myself. I would try to take only the good and blow the rest away. That is good advice!

Urge to what?

I am not a violent person, but sometimes, it takes a lot of control not to be. For example: I am driving down the road and someone gets within inches of my back bumper and starts flashing their lights to tell me to get out of their way. It is at that time that I can understand violence. The "urge to kill", stick out my tongue, or at least to slam on my brakes and cause them to panic does cross my mind.

I am not a jealous person but there are times when this is an honest emotion I will admit I have. When I see pictures of Elizabeth Taylor, Jane Fonda, and other beautiful people who number their birthdays higher than I do my own, I will admit to a tinge of jealousy of their youthful looks.

Envy is not one of those weaknesses that I would need to discuss with a good "shrink", even though I might admit to being envious at times. I do envy the person who always says and does the appropriate thing at the right time. I envy the person who is well-disciplined, efficient, well organized and who has never had the problem of being behind.

There have been times in recent years, when the crimes against and by children made me think that the end of time might be rapidly approaching. Like many of you, I have given much thought to the fact that children see so many acts of cruelty and violence on television that they may become immune to it in real life.

As I observe young people who spout their views concerning their rights to break the laws and find amusement at the cost of society, businesses, and innocent people as occur during Freaknik weekends, in Atlanta, I found that I was appalled at their attitudes of entitlement. But, all of these feelings take a back seat to the horror and disbelief we all share over the insanity of the Oklahoma bombing and the New York Trade Center.

Does it surprise us that America has people so filled with hate that they would plant bombs and fly airplanes into buildings to kill innocent people and helpless children? Is it beyond our imagination? And will we be surprised to see individuals against the death penalty for those people when they are brought to trial?

I can still be childlike.

"The glory of springtime is the same to all. But there are many different points of view. A child sees it best from the middle of a mud puddle."

A three year old discussing his mom with his teacher for his Mother's Day gift card said: "She likes to watch Okra on television." Another said his mom's favorite pastime was drinking adult drinks, while yet another little one told his teacher his mom liked to chew tobacco. " Can't fool a child!

Children have always fascinated me. Their innocence and their honesty are matchless. Why we allow them to grow out of those desirable traits into teenagers and adults is ridiculous, but we can't put a stop to growth.

Crawling through the tunnel and jumping in the air filled play structure has long been my "gift" to preschool children. Seeing an "old woman" crawling through the darken tunnel makes the children laugh but also gives them the courage to try it too. The jumping structure is another story all together.

I didn't even consider my size or the size of the opening and the fact that there were six other children in there jumping. Their immediate response was to attack the "old lady" and pull her down and stack kids on her. It worked like a charm. I fell down immediately, not by intention, and ten minutes later I managed to extricate myself and fall out the small opening to freedom.

Needless to say the children begged me to return to the play structure for another attack. I quickly found an avenue of escape and holding my hurting back I returned to the safety of the adult world of "watching" the fun.

As a grown up child I go to movies for kids if I can get one to accompany me so the movie managers don't keep an eye on me. I laugh at the antics of the characters and I can talk with some degree of familiarity to preschoolers about Power Rangers, Shreck, Digimon, and Yu-Gi-Oh!

On my computer there are games for our niece and nephew to play when they get bored at our house. After dark I sneak in and play a few games just so I can explain how to play them to Mary and Jacob. So far, they haven't caught on that I also like to try and better my score.

We often leave our childhood loves and laughs behind us as we travel into adulthood. The mud holes and running through the sprinklers and the fun and fantasy of childhood get lost in our memories. I try to capture those moments at times and relive them with my favorite little people.

We didn't have it so bad!

We always looked forward to summer with anticipation as well as fear. The last week of school was dreaded as we anticipated final exams. We lamented the fact that our year's average was not quite what we had hoped and we would have to take a final.

The teachers did not bless us with study sheets much less the answers. She might say, "You can expect this on the final." Or even if she said, "This might be on the final," we knew it most certainly would be. We might even study the whole year's information only to be asked one or two questions that took hours to finish. We would beg for multiple-choice questions only to be told there would be five discussion questions instead.

Nothing was "handed to us on a silver platter" as the old saying goes. Teachers gave assignments that were often ten pages hand written and if a page was not neat, that one had to be re-written. There were no computers with spell check and a dictionary was close at hand because misspelled words were not tolerated.

I dreaded all tests, knowing that I might disappoint my parents, my teachers, or myself. I didn't have a sibling close enough in age to make competition in the family, but I had cousins. All of them were boys, and girls knew they didn't really count when it came to grades.

I always felt like I should have done better during the year and final exams were my last chance to come out ahead. During the year, I consistently scored almost as well as most of the students in my classes, however, there were always the exceptions, the "brains" who always made perfect on tests.

Spelling finals would be a hundred words of those you most often misspelled all year long. Writing them a hundred times after a weekly test did not insure that you would spell it right on the test at the end. All of those rules of spelling such as "I" before "e" except after "c" and the exceptions to that rule would scurry through your brain and disappear on exam day.

Thinking back, our childhood was pretty good. We did not have the distraction of television or movies, or hanging out. We didn't have the constant distraction of video games and computer "my space" that took up all of our time. We could be really bored or we could do our chores and homework.

Young people today think we talk about hard times to let them know they have it easy. We talk about our growing up years to let them know that even under those circumstances we turned out pretty good. All those material objects they now enjoy are "gifts" from a generation that experienced the difficulties and came out on top.

When I pause to think of our soldiers in Iraq, I also pause and remember classmates who were in Korea and Vietnam. They didn't have emails and cell phones and families were not sure of their fates at all times. Families continue to enjoy the endeavors of generations of the past who turned out okay.

Mother was Adventurous

I would call Mother on the phone to check on her plans for the day. In her 70's she was a busy person and a trip to Cartersville was an hour's drive both ways. She worked at the church thrift shop, went to a Bible study, carried meals to shut-ins, and once a month she met, her sister, at the thrift shop to size and repair men's pants. Needless to say, I did not just drop in on her.

"Be sure and put your tool box in the car!" Always the handy fixer for Mother since the death of my Dad, she would wait for my visit to fix one thing or another. She was one of the most independent people I have ever known and I did not realize until much later that this was a real compliment to me. Allowing me to help her was one of the best parts of my visit.

I would tell her, "We are going to lunch somewhere, so you choose the place." Most often she would busy herself in the kitchen preparing a meal for the two of us so I could spend more time with her in between little jobs. If we did venture to a restaurant she would always order a hamburger. No matter how much was on the menu, she always "liked hamburgers better than anything".

Mom was an adventurer too. At age 65 she went with a group from her church to Bolivia. For many days she rode on the back of a pickup truck over narrow mountain roads and through creeks that were near impassable. Arriving in a small village the team of volunteers had special tasks and Mother's task was to help with the children, but others in the group knew that Mother could cook anything. On several occasions she made cakes with very few of the necessary ingredients.

As it turned out, the trip to Bolivia was a frightening adventure. Two weeks into the six- week stay the military took over the country and the American volunteers were arrested, hauled away in trucks and put into prisons. Several days later the American embassy forced the military to release them, but for many days we worried about her fate.

Mother kept newspaper clippings, cards from friends, letters, poems she had copied on envelopes, recipes in books she was reading, and a treasure of words here and there about her house. I inherited this trait from her. I am a well organized person but readily admit that I am first and foremost a "searcher". I know which room, which drawers, which cabinets, which boxes, general information about where a particular item should be. Once I begin a search, there appears to be no rhyme or reason to my organization, but like Mom, eventually I find whatever I am hunting.

During one of my search patterns one week I wasted a little time re-reading treasures from Mother's scrapbook. There among my collections were articles written about her after she was killed by an intruder in February 1989. The caption on one of the article was "she will be missed; her faithfulness, her love, her kindness, and her willingness to do for other people." Our parent leave us a legacy and with much pleasure we remember.

My Mother used to tell me…

When our children are young, every minute of the day could be called mothers' day. There is "Mother why can't I, why should I, can I have, will you let me?" Notice all are questions! Then there are the: "Ah Mom, I don't remember, I didn't do it, and she said it first."

The adolescent years are the "you didn't make my brother (sister) do it why do I have to?" The next few years are filled with "but it wasn't my fault; what's wrong with the way I look; and my room looks fine to me."

During this phase we moms find ourselves in the "pity group" because we do not have any intelligence and can't seem to understand what is going on around us. We can't understand the ridiculous styles, the lack of clothes that young people are wearing and our opinion on any subject is met with a look of pity because our minds have suddenly gone "bye-bye".

College years are filled with the usual, " I can get by with $20 but $50 would be better." Along with this mother's day expression is the one from college days that says it all, " if you can just wash them and have them ready Sunday afternoon!' Or better yet, "Why can't I wash the red shirt with the white clothes?"

The next mom phase is the one where we try to be friends with our children. We try to recapture our youth and attempt to play volley ball with them, we think we can do a run or a walk with them only to find out they are trying to slow their pace to meet ours. We schedule visits at their convenience and make sure we are available for performances and babysitting chores.

Often without warning, our roles change from independence to dependence on our children. Instead of them asking for permission we are asking for their help and we want to be available to help but we are physically or mentally unable to do so. They begin to worry about us rather than us worrying about them and convenience is tossed out the window because "Mom and Dad need me."

Our role of mother continues to change during the years of bringing up children until we pass into the "remember when" eras like our own mothers. We recall the advice she gave, pass it on to our children and wait until years later to hear them give the same advice to their children. We delight in recalling experiences with our own mother and hope that by some miracle we have impressed our own children in order for them to one day say: "My Mother used to tell me…."

Our children make us mothers in name only. Our devotion and dedication to the responsibilities of motherhood make us Mothers. I find myself saying these words often, "My Mother used to say!" Every day I recall all those special times with my Mom, hope you do too.

Parents Cast Long Shadows

Richard Eyre wrote: "Our parents cast long shadows over our lives. When we grow up, we imagine that we can walk in the sun, free of them. We don't realize, until it is too late, that we have no choice in the matter; they're always ahead of us."

In late winter and early spring, as the shrubs begin to bud and the bulbs, hidden deep in the ground, begin to push up through the dirt, I remember the long hard hours of work in the greenhouse with my parents. I remember saying over and over, under my breath of course, that I would never, ever be caught planting flowers, fertilizing plants, and worrying about a drought. However, over the years I have "eaten" those words many times.

I catch myself saying "Mother use to say" and "Daddy could do anything". I find myself wishing that my Dad could give me the answer to certain questions or that I could just ask Mother about this problem or that one. When I browse through a hardware department I find myself thinking, my Dad would love this new gadget or that new tool. When I watch Grandmothers with grandchildren I recall vividly the way Mother enjoyed hers. I realize more and more each day that many shadows are cast over my life by the memories made by my parents.

Perhaps, it is a shame that children and young adults do not understand this concept early in their lives and take full advantage of the talents and wisdom of their parents. Perhaps, it would be good if teenagers could just skip over that time when Mom and Dad know very little, if anything at all. Age-old wisdom proves beyond a shadow of a doubt that every age has to do their own choosing and their own maturing. For parents and for children, the transition to maturity seems to take forever.

I hear young parents say: "I didn't understand what my Father meant until I had children of my own." I listen with interest to the mother of a teenager remark that she now understands comments her own mother made to her when she was that same age. And in the same sentence, these individuals will continue with the words: "I wish that I had listened more often to what my parents said."

So often in life we fail to answer those questions that are most important to us as individuals: "where am I going, and how do I get there?" My own idea of these questions concerns us personally and gives us the perspective into what we will be and by what means we are influenced to be the person we want to be. If we fail to recognize the influence of our parents and the contributions made by our heritage and our environment, then we fail to realize what Eyre meant when he said: "We carry our parents within us all our lives - in the shape of our face, the way we walk, the sound of our voice, our skin, our hands, our heart. We try all our lives to separate ourselves from them, and only when they are gone do we find we are indivisible."

How did you grow up?

"We do not choose to be born. We do not choose our parents. We do not choose the circumstances of our upbringing." These words of Joseph Epstein caused me to stop long enough to think about the advantages and disadvantages of my upbringing.

I grew up in a small town where everyone knew their neighbors and the first question asked by most newcomers was: "Now who are your parents?" This of course led to all the facts concerning our place in society, where we attended church, and what our father did for a living. Needless to say, our place in the realm of the newcomer's list of acquaintances was determined by our answers.

As I think back there were several times that my choice of friends meant a raised eyebrow from my parents or my relatives. They could not understand why with all the friends I could choose I picked a person who had few or no friends. I would choose to sit at their table in the lunchroom or in the desk right by their side. Places on the society roll meant very little to me.

I suppose it was my upbringing. We had very little in terms of financial wealth. Just like everyone else we had ration stamps and hand-me-down clothes and shoes that were often too small for our feet.

On one side of the family our grandparents were farmers and had plenty to eat, but they rode to town on Saturday in the farm truck if they went at all. On the maternal side our grandparents worked in the Goodyear Mills in Cartersville. My grandfather distinguished himself as a supervisor in the carding room. Don't ask me what a carding room was because that was not part of my growing up education.

You see, this was during the war and everyone had a job to do. Women who had never worked outside the home went to work in factories and grandmothers kept the children. We were very much aware that having "stuff" was not as important as being loved for who and what we were as individuals.

We did not choose our lifestyle or our parents but for sure we were luckier than most kids. We had parents who expected us to be an example for other children, to mind our manners, to behave, and "if you can't say something nice don't say anything at all."

Our upbringing carried us through the troublesome years as teenagers when neighbors reported every little infraction of the rules they knew our parents had for us. Our teachers reported any and all straying outside the guidelines and we could expect retribution from our parents when we got home.

I did not choose my parents or the circumstances of my upbringing, I'm just happy about the choice that was made for me.

LaVerne was a Tough Bully!

She was a sixth grader; a red headed, smart-aleck, know-it-all named LaVerne. Yes, her name really was LaVerne, no joke. This was my first experience with the term "groupie" as LaVerne gathered a bunch of girls who tagged along in her presence. These girls thought they were as tough as their leader. Bullies they are called now.

I was only in the fourth grade but I knew that LaVerne was not as tough as she wanted everyone to believe. She didn't know everything either and her report card was definite proof. She rode my bus and lived just up the hill from us. Once her cronies were gone she lost a lot of her superiority and was a right decent person.

The only time LaVerne and I had any problems was when she would try to bully me. If I couldn't ignore her sly remarks about me, or what I was wearing, I gave her the look that said "I know something about you too". One thing for sure, on a scale of one to ten, we both registered about two in "bully tactics".

My best friend was a chubby little girl that didn't have many friends. She was the object of many practical jokes and was constantly suffering from one humiliation or another, usually at the hands of LaVerne or her cronies.

The incident that stands out in my mind was just another of those pranks that were played on my best friend. As tears sprung to her eyes, anger filled mine. I suppose it was the smirk on LaVerne's face that did it. That "I dare you to hit me" stare made my hands curl into fists. The first lick was going to be mine this time.

I put everything I had into that hit knowing it would be my first and last one. My lucky punch connected with her lip and that was my last punch. Her first blow took me down as it caught my eye and the white immediately turned red. The fight stopped as quick as it started.

There was no doubt that I would be in trouble when I got home that day. My parents forbade fighting with friends and that red eye was an unmistakable sign of a fight I had lost. This event sticks in my mind as a poor solution to a problem, but the aftermath of standing up for friends has been a very good guideline for me.

Anger often takes over logic in many situations. Only when I became an adult did I realize that those cycles of fighting when we are young spill over into families. Abusive husbands punch and curse children and wives. Abusive women embarrass their children in public, and on and on the stories go.

Too bad there are more LaVernes in the world than there are peacemakers. To bad everyone did not get a red eye punch when they were young and could learn the lesson about fighting. Too bad everyone couldn't hear my Mother say with authority, "Sticks and stones will break your bones but words will never hurt you." I still have a hard time believing that one.

The title of teacher is earned.

I had all the answers on my first day as a teacher! I had just finished a college class of instruction on how to be an effective teacher. Snug under my arm was all my notes from classes in science, geography, math, and how to teach reading. With all the know-how a young person could have, I walked confidently into the classroom.

There in front of me sat 36 bright faces. I misinterpreted their eager looks to mean they were ready for the new teacher to begin instructing them in the academia of sixth grade education. Naïve as I was, it took me all of five minutes to realize I had seriously mistaken their looks of anticipation.

By noontime of the first day I knew my work was cut out for me. Those eager students had me in tow as we headed for the lunchroom. They were smart, real smart! They knew that I was over-confident and over-whelmed and they definitely had the upper hand since they out numbered me 36-1. By the end of the day the word exhaustion did not fully explain the condition of my body.

I suppose the "look of desperation" on my face registered with the other teachers on my hall. Just down the way a few doors stood a special lady who had taught me in the fourth grade. Miss Kennedy had a knowing grin on her face that said volumes on "you don't have a clue, do you?"

Next-door was Mrs. Ashlee Johnson in fifth grade and across the hall was Mrs. Warlick in a third grade room. They were about the age of my Mother or a little younger. When they had finished leading their students out to go home, they gathered in my room to check on the "know-it-all" college student who had finished her first day.

I will never forget how they sympathized with my plight of being in charge of one of the smartest groups of children to ever go through Cherokee Avenue Elementary School. You see, they had taught this same classroom of students the previous years and they understood how much attention had to be paid to keeping them busy and interested.

I was the youngster in that school for two years before moving out of town. Those "seasoned" teachers had to continuously reach out to the youngster in their midst. Their expertise was more important than any class I took in college. I found out from them that teaching was more than knowing material and having plans, it also included the love of teaching and that love is only acquired with practice.

Theodore Roosevelt wrote: "Teach boys and girls alike that they are not to look forward to lives spent in avoiding difficulties; teach them that work for themselves and others is not a curse but a blessing." Those teachers helped me, a young beginner, to appreciate and receive the blessings of being a teacher.

English and etiquette!

Mrs. Tripp was my English teacher, but she also taught journalism in my high school. She had a unique name, Jewell Tripp, but in her later years, as an old maid teacher, she changed her status by marrying Mr. Sewell and her name was even more unique as Jewell Sewell.

Mrs. Sewell was a stickler for English grammar as was her predecessors in high school. Miss Gemes grilled us our entire eighth grade year on the finer points of diagramming a sentence. She insisted that we not only diagram them but that we be able to tell the part of speech for each word, as well as, how the words were used in the sentence.

Needless to say we were only able to cover about five sentences a day and we dreaded our turn at the board. If there was an adjective or adverb in the sentence we also had to tell what word it modified and what question it answered. The worst English mistake we could make was to end a sentence with a preposition. That was an infraction that would send these teachers into an English tirade.

The English language and the proper use of words have come a long way in the last few years. The use of, *for*, and *to* at the end of a sentence is no big deal. Having a subject and a verb in every sentence does not seem necessary anymore. All those rules that took us years to memorize seem as useless today as the geometry and physics classes.

There are many teacher related lessons that have stuck with me. Mrs. Sewell said a good editorial in a newspaper should make the reader think or ask questions after it was read. Perhaps this is a good reason to respond to any editorial that pricks your mind or imagination.

Another valuable lesson was taught by Mrs. Elliott. She was at least 100 pounds "soaking wet with a brick in each hand" as the saying goes. She was maybe five feet tall, maybe less, but she stood her ground with the biggest and best of the giant football players in our school.

Mrs. Elliott was hardheaded when it came to manners. Not opening a door for a lady to enter was particularly aggravating to her. She would grasp the arm of a monstrously big ball player, spin him around to face her, and when her tirade on good manners was over, the young man never forgot the encounter.

Needless to say, teachers who invoked their ideas of right and wrong behavior and their learning patterns still have an effect on my personality. Those teachers of long ago could put fear in our hearts with a look of disapproval. No corporal punishment was necessary; they commanded our respect and our parents insisted they received it.

I can still picture those teachers in my bank of fond memories. I often make English grammar mistakes and forget the perfect rules of etiquette, but some of their lessons have not rubbed off entirely.

Are children just smarter?

I made this statement: "Children are not smarter than they have ever been, they just have more information to absorb!" Speak to any teacher and they will attest to the fact that children have always been smart. Teachers will tell you of many children they have taught that presented a real challenge because of their brilliance, their curiosity, and their ability to absorb facts.

The emphasis of my statement was that children today are overwhelmed, and often traumatized by an abundance of information. Sometimes we give them so much to learn that they are reeling from too much to know before they are ready to handle it. A child asks a simple question about the birds and the bees and we give them the whole reproductive process. They may ask why a river is dirty and we give them the whole ecology bit.

The computer age is upon them and the Internets, cyber nets, and what-nets, are available with a click of a switch and a surge of electricity. Unlike my generation, who had to go to the library and check out a book and read it, our children are mastering the art of countless resources available through a phone or cable line.

With the new age of ease and comfort on the computer, educators are challenged to make sure children also knows the basic information necessary about math, English, and other subjects in order to use a computer to its utmost purpose.

Mistakes of the past have taught that shortcuts in education do not always work. We have re-thought the open classrooms and put the walls up again. We have stopped allowing children to learn by counting on their fingers and the phonics reading (called the "Blue Back Speller Method' in my Mother's day) has proven to be the most effective way to learn to read.

Even now educators would like to re-consider corporal punishment. Society itself should stop and re-evaluating its stand on many issues. With the increase in the prison population and the crime rate among teens on the increase, we have begun to re-examine closely the lack of discipline, the need for discipline, and the absence of discipline in the homes, in the schools, and in our nation.

Children have more information than parents had at the same age but that does not mean that they are smarter, it just means they have more information. Smart has always been around. It isn't a new item in classrooms, and it still presents a challenge for teachers each and every day. Let's not be caught up in "smarts" and forget the child underneath.

Moments of Happiness

She is just over two years old and at times she can be a little bit pouty. I've been trying to win her over for several months because she is the child of one of my favorite moms. Anna would often look at me like she didn't want me to speak and would pout just enough to make me want to win her over even more.

I believe what finally worked was the laughter. She had been cooped up in a room with other children for over an hour and had just about enough of cooperating. She looked really stressed out if indeed a two year old can be stressed. All she wanted was a kind face and someone to pick her up from the confusion around her. I was available and in a few moments we were laughing at each other, not just giggles, but real belly laughing. Instant gratification it could be called.

For a child, happiness is a magical quality. They are delighted by an adult who will slide down the slide, giggle and laugh on command, or just do something silly with them. They can experience lows at any time but can be tempted to climb out of their pout sessions with some coaxing. This is a challenge for adults who may see a child as difficult, but when coaxing makes a laugh session with the child it is quite rewarding.

In the passage from young child to the teenage years the concept of happiness and laughter change. The embarrassment of peers causes laughter; the teachers who should be respected for caring and concern are treated with grins and laughs, often behind their backs, of course. Teens define happiness with words like excitement, popularity, and whether their face is free of teenage acne. Their happy moments often escape their attention because their definitions are forever changing with their moods.

Adults find that the things that bring them the most joy and happiness are also attached to responsibilities. Marriage, children, homes, and jobs are happy areas but carry with them the risk of loss. Lynn Peters wrote: "Love may not last, sex isn't always good, loved ones die. For adults, happiness is complicated."

I added up moments of happiness and pleasures from yesterday. I had an hour of uninterrupted time with a good book and quiet reflections without a phone ringing. I walked for several miles on a warm day, I was hugged around the knees by several waist-high friends at the preschool, and I enjoyed conversations with very good friends over dinner. I watched three squirrels chase each other around the big oak tree just outside my study window and watched as the two little dogs that belong to neighbors leaped up the tree in pursuit.

While happiness can be more complex for us as adults, the solution is still the same as ever. Happiness isn't about what happens to us but it is rather what we perceive happens to us. It is the knack of finding something positive in the negative and not wishing for what we don't have, but enjoying what we do possess. A good example is a child's acceptance and her laughter.

Peer pressure or life styles?

"Why are young people so angry these days," the woman remarked. Her friend responded, "If you had to wear those big soled shoes and baggy pants all day to be in style, you'd be mad too."

Anger in our young people is not as simple as clothing styles and peer pressure, it is much more complex. Wrong choices made by young people are much more serious problems. From the young teenage parents who did accept responsibility for a wrong act to those who sought abortions in sleazy dark rooms; from high school pranks that turned bad and ruined reputations and careers to high speed automobiles that missed dangerous curves and lives were lost; young people have always had choices that they had to be made.

Peer pressure is still exactly what a young person wants to make of it. They can allow the callous behavior of insecure people to put them down and belittle them or they can realize the problem is not their own but it is instead the problem of the one harassing. They can go with the crowd, or they can stand firm in their decisions to do what is right. However, choosing a side is often one of the most difficult and painful experiences of their young life.

I lived on the "wrong side of the tracks" growing up in Cartersville, or so I thought. It was not until many years later that I discovered the classmates who lived across town had just as many problems growing up as we did. Their "wonderful lives" were filled with disappointments, frustrations and keeping up a front was as difficult for them as our not caring attitude was for us on the other side of the "tracks".

What happens to our young people? Is it too much too soon? Is it expecting them to act like adults before they have the maturity to be adults? Is it unrestricted freedom and more money than they need? Is it less parental supervision or just a lack of constructive family conversations? Is it less to do and more time on their hands? Is it the job that keeps the grades up or jobs that keep the grades down?

The media continues to frighten us with their coverage of the possibilities of teen violence. Parents fear their children are in constant danger in our schools and educators scramble to buy metal detectors, hire security guards, and monitor halls with sophisticated cameras. The airwaves are filled with talk show hosts with all the professional experts who have all the right answers, but the scare goes on and on. Is it time to accept the fact that we have angry teenagers and search for the reasons why they are angry? Seems the time is always right to do just that!

Our Time is a Priceless Commodity

According to pollster Louis Harris, "Time may have become the most precious commodity in the land." You may argue that point if you have filled a gas tank on your car lately. It is even difficult for some of us to remember when gas cost less than a dollar a gallon. It is even more difficult to recall when a dollar's worth of gas would cruise us around the courthouse square all Sunday afternoon.

Back to the subject! We do not have less time. There are still 24 hours, seven days a week, and with all those labor saving devices, how can we not have more time? Cars go faster, shopping with self-serve registers is quicker, and cell phones make calling ahead so convenient. How come we seem to have less time?

We are now into the quick time of a school year. Children get out in June and start back in August. Correct that statement to read, "Kids get out in September, October, November, December, and so forth." Do you get the picture? Of course, it use to be easier for parents and child keepers for school to last nine months and be out for three.

An ordinary day for us might be a few minutes, to several hours of rest in the parking lots we know as four-lanes. A few moments of rest might be while we wait at a county or city park for a child to finish some sporting practice. Another time of rest might be in a dentist or doctor's office, but seldom do we call these moments a time of rest.

We have replaced equipment with time saving devices. Offices have copiers instead of those purple sheets. There are computers instead of typewriters. There is email instead of letters diligently typed by competent stenographers. Files are now on a small round disk or a square one. These can even be saved on a small device carried on a key ring.

Microwaves, coffeemakers, frozen meals in a bag, fast foods, all were to give us more free time. They have certainly failed in this goal. Now we zip here and there trying to catch up with our over-scheduled schedule. Labor saving, perhaps! Time saving, not really! Money saving, not in the least! Work more, cost more, save more?

Louis Harris was correct when he said that time was a precious commodity. It has become a commodity that is very hard to capture. It is used up each day by obligations and schedules and timesaving devices. To quote another writer, "Free time gained by us by technology didn't make us relax; it made us run." Makes me tired to think about it.

Stay Within the Lines!

Mary loved to use crayons and each time she sat at the table with a coloring book her instructions were the same: "Stay in the lines!" At her young age she would select a color and with it held firmly in her fist she would scrub the crayon all over the picture. As her small motor skills developed, her dexterity and her listening skills improved, she began to follow directions and her coloring book skills improved. She learned to stay within the lines.

Our lives are like the instructions for the coloring book, stay within the lines! Parents instruct, teach, and encourage children to stay within the lines. Schools, churches, and society instruct, teach, and make demands that we follow directions and stay within the lines. Laws, rules of conduct, procedures and instructions are encountered every day, but how often do we fail to adhere to the rules and stay within the lines?

Most of us follow the basic ones such as not parking in the handicap spaces, fire lanes, and maintaining the posted speed limit. But little things become bigger ones as we ignore the lines or push them further out. Shopping carts are left out of racks damaging cars; customers do not put unwanted items back on shelves where they belong; people smoke in non-smoking areas; and even more dangerous are impatient motorist who pass cars on yellow lines or in turning lanes and zigzag across lanes at high speeds.

We transfer disrespect for the lines through our attitudes and teach our children disrespect for rules of conduct. We try to encourage good behavior by saying: "If you will behave while we are in the store I'll buy you something!" But we do not enforce our rules because temper tantrums are ignored in stores. We accept as commonplace inappropriate behavior, and we expect nothing better.

Some lines are unreal. A person who can throw, bounce, kick, or hit a ball makes millions to play games while people starve and sleep on streets. When poverty, hatred, disease and child abuse are on the rise and organizations must beg for funding, what has happened to the lines? When youngsters find perverse pleasure in belittling, abusing, harassing, taunting, and bullying and this behavior is allowed to flourish unchecked because of lawsuits and unfair laws, are we outside the lines? When computer games of violence cease to be games, and the lines of communication are severed, have the lines disappeared.

How do we teach, or learn, or instruct others that staying within the lines is important? How do we become mature adults who will admit our mistakes, accept the responsibility for our actions, and not shift blame to our parents or a scapegoat? When will we begin to recognize the difference in the lines of equally and the ones of preferential treatment?

Staying in the lines may not be your way or the way you want your children to act but what happens when the lines are forcefully moved and endanger your lives? What happens when you cross the path of another who has ignored the lines as in the case of drunk drivers? What happens to society when the lines are erased one by one and decency, fair play, self control and the law can no longer protect and defend us. Have we forgotten how to stay within the lines?

Has Good Manners Disappeared?

What is the last thing you say to a child before you go into a one hour church service? The correct answer is: "Have you been to the bathroom?" Parents have lost this question somewhere along the way. The bathroom brigade during most church services, or any other event, has grown to countless numbers. Not only are the ministers or speakers distracted, but everyone else is temporarily distracted by the up and down activities of both children and adults, who forgot to go before they sat down.

Who changed the rules and did I miss getting a copy? Since when do we allow children to disrupt teachers in classrooms without fear of punishment? Since when do we frown on anyone who expects children to regard rules of etiquette and good manners as essential to learning self-control? Why do we punish good students by allowing the disruptive and misbehaving kids to have the upper hand?

I could have left the half-filled shopping cart right there in the line and walked out of the store, but that would not have been nice. After ten minutes of listening to a three year old pitch a fit in the grocery store, crying loudly, and at one point, laying in the floor while being ignored by her parents, I nearly had enough. Other customers in my age range rolled their eyes upward, frowned, shook their heads in amazement, and like me, tried to stand the noise long enough to have purchases checked out. Who changed the rules about children should be seen and not heard? How do parents stand this type behavior?

Even today, I have difficulty with adults who have lost the art of politeness. I find it hard to accept that the only people who say thank you are those who occasionally say it at a check out counter. I still cannot understand how politeness and good manners have gotten a bad name among the younger generation. Since when is telling it like it is and saying whatever you think called honesty? Whatever happened to "silence is golden"? Or better yet, "People may think you a fool, but don't open your mouth and remove all doubt!"

I often recall an incident with a very young child who had learned well one particular guideline from her parents: "If you cannot say something nice, don't say anything." The child was playing while her father finished some work in his office. A very large gentleman entered, overalls, old hat, and with only one tooth, front, top and middle of his mouth. To the four year old he was a scary sight and she immediately ran to her father and buried her head in his chest. With prompting, the child raised her head and true to her upbringing she remarked: "Daddy, isn't his tooth pretty?"

Somebody needs to find that old set of rules again because we are rapidly losing the framework for kindness, discipline, and good manners. Learning begins at an early age, sitting still for one hour in church is a good place to start.

Can Johnny Read?

We hear a lot today about how Johnny can't read, how he can't write, how he can't make change for a dollar, but the most disturbing aspect of Johnny's learning is his inability to control his threats, his anger, and his behavior. Psychologists, school officials, government and church authorities are well aware that there is a more serious problem affecting our children than their reading or writing skills, distinguishing the difference between right and wrong.

Children who have been so angry that they have killed teachers and classmates have stunned the nation. Each night we could read about another child making threats of bodily harm and carrying them out. . The news media is filled with example after example of the uncontrolled rage of children, teen gangs, young adults, and even young married people, who have committed what were once "unthinkable" crimes of violence.

There is a deep moral confusion in today's society that we can add to the list of educational problems. There is a definite lack of knowledge concerning manners, morals, and standards of behavior. Young people who should be well aware of the Ten Commandments, the consequences of legal and illegal behavior, are thumbing their noses at what is right and wrong, choosing to display behavior that is unacceptable and often punishable for a lifetime.

They believe the only way to receive attention is killing classmates and teachers. Certainly there is violence on television but unsupervised viewing of the violence can be blamed on parents not children and television executives. The truth is that parental guidance, supervision and instructions are missing in too many homes. Parents are struggling to maintain two cars, well furnished homes, and making their careers a priority and leaving the job of teaching their children right from wrong to school teachers, scout leaders, coaches, and anyone else who will make the attempt.

But the question still remains: " who is to blame for the moral and ethical standards in today's society?" We began with "if it feels good do it" and have progressed to "disregard the consequences if you are angry". We, as a society, have tied the hands of school officials in discipline, teaching behavior standards, and dealing with the complexity of educational and ethical requirements. We have dumped the problems of our world into the laps of schools and churches and take no responsibility for our own creations, our children.

What will it take to make us realize that our children are more important? What will it take to make us understand that when the restraints of discipline are released the child is un-tethered in his behavior and violent acts? What is it going to take to make us acknowledge that unsupervised and undisciplined children are in potential danger to themselves and others?

Heroes for Today

"Faster than a speeding bullet, more powerful than a locomotive, able to lift tall buildings in a single bound. Look! Up in the sky! It's a bird, it's a plane, it's Superman".

"From out of the pass comes the thundering hoof beats of the great horse Silver, the Lone Ranger rides again. Return with us now to those thrilling days of yesteryears as the masked rider of the plains leads his fight for law and order."

Do these words sound familiar? Do they return you to a past when heroes did not climb into bed with a pretty girl in every episode? Do you remember the thrill of these radio programs: The Shadow, The Invisible Man, and the Green Hornet? Can you picture in your mind these characters: Roy Rogers, Hopalong Cassidy, Lone Ranger, and Poncho and the Cisco Kid? Can you recall the story lines and the endings when good always won and immediately the children imitated the actions and behavior of their heroes?

A comment within my hearing made me realize that "sex sells" everything from cars to cereal on primetime television and that every sitcom depicts the decay of morality in one-way or another. Strange relationships within and without the bonds of marriage, vulgar and crude language just short of X rated; and implied and depicted sexual conducts are the basis of many programs.

One program that was refreshing was Touched by an Angel, but it was soon cut. Each time the program went off the comment at our house was the same: "I cannot believe they allow such a good program to air on television!" This was a program that used the word God, showed right from wrong, and did not resort to profanity, vulgarity or violence to make a point. It was as far removed from sex topics as a program could get.

What caused us as a society to be so consumed with the cults and idolatry of sex and immorality? Who decided for America that our morals were such that we wanted to see, hear and read about subjects that were once taboo and were discussed only in the privacy of our home? Are we as a nation so accepting of low moral standards that we are apathetic about what is shown to children and teenagers during the day and early evening hours? Do we condone these programs by supporting their sponsors?

Think about the programs in the last 10-15 years that are still popular. Mayberry with Andy and Barney are on each evening. I Love Lucy still has a big following. The reruns of old movies command big audiences and a hug and kiss depicts the extent of the sexual encounters of the characters. Variety and entertainment shows used to be the norm for sponsors of programs during primetime. "What sells" is now the norm, or is it?

We may not see results of this decline in standards of behavior for several years. We may not admit the impact of this attitude change on the younger generation until they reach adulthood, but, are we not now focusing the responsibility for the present day problems on the freedom and feel good attitude of the 60's, and 70's? Is that the cause or the excuse?
*Written in 1995

Reunions and Homecomings

A phone call reminded me that the Homecoming Services would be at the church where I grew up. It has been years since I have been to this event and plans, already made, prevented me from attending this year.

On our Memorial Day "ride" we passed several small country churches and the cemeteries had been well tended and graves were marked with fresh colors of spring. Off to the sides of many churches the arbors over picnic tables still held the remains of dinner and people stood or sat in small groups reminiscing about the past.

I was reminded of the many summer events we attended growing up. There were the usual homecoming services but the family reunions, those are the memories I now cherish.

Mother's sisters were never as interesting as they were when they got together at a reunion. It seemed that they evoked an endless stream of laughter and funny expressions when they joined forces. Their recall of childhood antics and adventures made us youngsters wonder why they did not allow this humor to appear when they were at home.

There were lots of cousins of every age and disposition. There were first, second and third cousins and the expression "twice removed" never did quite make sense to me. As a child I could envision someone being bodily taken away twice only to return like a bad penny.

There were the usual accidents that occurred with so many people sitting or standing in groups of two or more. Children were running around chasing each other, and some grown up would wind up having his or her feet knocked out from under them by a fast moving child. One child, usually in our family, would get hurt and have to go for stitches or a cast at a nearby hospital.

The ride to the reunion location always took forever but the ride home was quiet and peaceful. The adults were talked out and the children were worn out. We would get home and Daddy would carry the younger children to bed and Mother would wash their feet just before she tucked them in and gave them a kiss.

I can still envision the place where we went every summer for a family reunion. I can see my granddaddy in his black suit and tie even though it was way too hot for a suit. I can see us in our Sunday best clothes waiting patiently for kinfolk to pat us on the head and tell us how much we had grown.

Aunt Frances' coconut cake and Mother's caramel cake ranked so far above the "best" classification that I don't consider them in my choosing the best part of the day. The best part of the day was the moment Mother called to us and said we could now put on our play clothes.

Dirt Beads and truck wagons

As I washed a "string of dirt beads" from under Jacob's neck, I recalled a time long ago when my younger brother, his dad, sported several rings of dirt around his neck at the end of the day. We all played hard and dirty when we were growing up. The only games we had were the ones we invented, and the more inventive, the dirtier we seemed to get.

Our favorite sport was racing. My Dad had made us a wagon from spare airplane parts. The wheels were the rear wheels from a small Piper Cub that belonged to my Uncle CJ. They were filled with ball bearings and they would roll faster than the wheels on the wagons of the other boys and girls.

The wagons were called "truck wagons", why, I do not know! I don't recall that term ever being explained to me. But, truck wagons we had, and a path was carved out through the woods behind our house. Down between the trees and undergrowth we had a place to race these wagons and someone always sported scraped elbows and legs.

We were fearless in our three-wheeled wagon. I didn't tell you about the three wheels, did I? Well, there was one on the front and Daddy had devised a steering pipe to move the front wheel for turns. Of course, there was one handicap. Even though the wheels were faster on our wagon, sharp turns would result in an immediate spill.

The wagon, constructed of metal from an old wrecked plane, meant that when it landed on top of you there was sure to be some damage to your body. The sides were about two inches high and falling out was a sure response to a spill but another one would be those two inches making tremendous bruises on legs, arms and bodies.

By the end of the day we were all covered in dirt and debris from spills and slides through the woods. The bruises and scrapes would begin to hurt and we would dread the bath we would need before bedtime. The rings around our necks were not the only rings of dirt we would sport after racing truck wagons all day. There were also rings around the bathtub.

The worst accident was one that involved a boy who lived next door to us. He was not very good controlling the three wheeled wagon as he tried to guide it between two trees. His legs were bent at the knees and stuck out on each side of the wagon. Going between the trees took the skin off his legs from knees to beyond.

I can almost hear the scream of torture that night as he sunk slowly into the tub of water. Of course, he didn't really scream because he didn't want his mom to know he had been out playing that afternoon. He should have been practicing his piano lessons like he was supposed to be. Oh well, he still tried many more times to get the steering down on that three wheel wagon.

Are you taking a hamster to camp meeting?

"You sure do have a big hamster," I told a young man as he carted eight bales of cedar shavings to his truck. He smiled and said it was so much easier and sanitary to use cedar shavings in the "tent" at Holbrook Campground in Cherokee County, Georgia than those from a sawmill.

This year many people are preparing earlier for camp meetings than in years past. Schools are beginning sooner due to schedules and holidays interspersed into the required 180 day school year. The old rule of third weekend of July or the first week of August are no longer the annual meetings dates.

No matter what the dates are, the preparations for "tenting" at local campgrounds are the same. The floors have to be cleaned and the varmints removed from their winter spaces and new shavings are put in place. The appliances are either hauled in or they are cleaned and checked out after a winter's reprieve.

Bicycles and tricycles, games, and all sorts of paraphernalia are hauled in for the kids' entertainment and the adults peace of mind during the day. It will be an exciting time for all when the crowd gathers for worship in the big arbors.

My favorite story of camp meetings is one from Pine Log Campground between Cartersville and Fairmount, Georgia. It seems that the roof on the arbor needed to be replaced and the trustees of the campground were having trouble raising enough money for the task. Putting heads together they decided to invite the Methodist Bishop, Arthur J. Moore to make a pitch about this problem.

Bishop Moore was always known by Methodist as a man of strategies and innovative methods of accomplishing impossible tasks. He was scheduled for the Sunday morning worship service and the arbor was packed and overflowing for his visit. Everyone was dressed to a "t" for the visit by the Bishop.

Bishop Moore started his message by proclaiming his delight in the blessings the members of the congregation had received. He had counted the number of fine automobiles in the yard and estimated the cost of each, totaling the cost. He bragged on the lovely hats of the women and how his own wife would have paid a certain amount for a hat similar to theirs.

With each item he called a blessing, he put a price to the amount of money represented under the arbor. He added up his assessments and continued to add shoes, suits, children's clothes and etc until he made an accumulated guess of the wealth of the listeners present for that morning's service.

As the ushers came forward for the morning offering, Bishop Moore said since God had blessed everyone so well he was sure they would want to contribute generously to the fund to re-roof the arbor before the next annual meeting When the offering was counted there was more than enough to replace the roof. Sometimes we must be prompted to count our blessings. True story? I think so!

Baptizing by Dunking

In the summer of 2007, our state experienced a severe drought. Discussing the water restrictions with a minister friend recently, he related his latest joke. He said the restrictions were so bad that the Baptist had gone to "sprinkling", the Methodist were using a washrag and the Presbyterians were giving rain checks."

This gave me reason to remember the events of the summers I enjoyed as a child when going swimming was a real adventure. There were no subdivisions with swimming pool amenities and Lake Allatoona was years away from completion in our area.

On very hot days we had the garden hose and running around in as few clothes as possible was a treat. We didn't have the fancy swimsuits, goggles, and paraphernalia it takes to go swimming now. Quite often we would get the big galvanized laundry tub and take turns in it, and that was fun only for a short time.

Going to the creek near the house was the adventure. This was a special treat because there was enough water for everyone to get soaked more than once. There were often times when we were very young that bathing attire was not necessary. The boys would get in the creek, turn their backs and the girls would get into the water. This was all under the keen supervision of our mothers.

Spring and summer revivals in all the churches meant that there would be baptizing events throughout the summer. Being a Methodist and just being sprinkled with water did not always satisfy converts and the entire congregation would meet at the creek for a Sunday afternoon baptizing.

There was one creek that was the choice of most churches because the shore sloped down easily and the bottom was fairly level. Another advantage was the water was deep enough for the minister to stand waist deep in water that made the "dunking" easier for him.

All the ladies would be dressed in white dresses and the men in their white shirts and any color pants. Many churches even had a supply of white gown like robes for their baptizings. My fear was always that someone would drown because the minister couldn't get him or her back up after they leaned them backwards. I have to admit I never did see a drowning of a baptized Christian.

There are many churches in the county that still maintain their pools for this special event. Some of the pools are on the outside and the later churches incorporated the pools into the sanctuaries. I am sure that baptismals still hold the same importance in the manmade pools but the fascination of the event in the creeks has to be a major memory for many. Even watching from the sidelines of the bank was an exceptional time for me.

Dirt Roads

"Too many dirt roads have been paved," writes Paul Harvey. These words brought back last week's column about the disappearance of clotheslines. Pavement is everywhere we look. Growth, development, population explosion, travel, and congestion have replaced the dirt roads. Some of us miss those simple thrills of life, but not enough to relive the past.

Paul Harvey says the era of the dirt roads taught many valuable lessons. Being cooped up in a hot dusty car made us appreciate shade trees and lemonade. Children learned that bad words tasted like soap, and we didn't have something to eat or drink until we got home or to our destination. A visit by family or friends on Sunday afternoon was a real treat.

During the dirt road era there were no drive by shootings because the cloud of dust announced the arrival of any vehicle and the dogs did the welcome attack. No one tailgated unless they wanted a mouthful of dirt or a rock through their windshield. People didn't worship their cars more than their kids and precious funds were not spent on wash and wax jobs. A stop in the creek did the cleanup for funerals and such.

We now have a nation of bored children who do not know how to have fun in the hot sun of summer vacation. They are addicted to air-conditioned rooms with television, games, and one or both parents on duty to plan fun and excitement for them, "taxi" them from place to place until teachers take over again next week.

I wonder if children know about catching fireflies or tying string to June bugs legs? Do they know about building a clubhouse out of pine needles, making moss hats, blowing dandelions or constructing truck wagons? Can they make believe they are pirates, soldiers, and magicians? Do they play outside until exhausted and they find rest under a shade tree?

This may be a southern thing, but we enjoyed family reunions on a hot, sticky far away campground. There was a dusty ride that took forever but when we arrived there were more cousins than we ever knew we had, and aunts and uncles everywhere. The food was awesome, fried chicken, pork chops, coconut cake, pecan pies, you name it someone specialized in its making.

The month of August started with camp meetings and I recall the times of the past with dirt roads, revivals in the arbor, saw dust floors, and services three times a day. Children knew the pleasures of simple play and their parents and grandparents were present to instruct them in proper behavior and manners.

We now have roads to everywhere and our lives are hurried and filled with pressing obligations. Speed, convenience, progress, labor saving, time management, acquisition of luxuries, quick food, and instant gratification, are words of the present. But some people still like to remember the dirt road era.

August 11, 2002

Time traveling

Don't you just love to time travel, to venture down back roads of your mind to locations of your childhood or teenage years? Don't you just love seeing the faces and places of the past come alive in your mind's eye? Isn't it a constant adventure to travel through the pleasant and meaningful times of your memory?

The train tracks were within walking distance of the house where we lived. The trestle ran high in the air above the creek where on very hot summer days we could go wading, or swimming if we were lucky enough to know how to do that exercise. Underwear was the swim gear of the day and the water was muddy enough that there was little to be seen with coed swimming.

Bicycles were the dreams of kids in our neighborhood. They were passed down just like clothing between kinfolk's and were in a constant state of disrepair. Fenders were bent, tires were thread bare, but they provided hours of camaraderie and laughter for all of us. With each "pass down" one more child could join the entourage of cyclists.

Our neighborhoods were safe. The bicycle gang was all laughter, excitement, and careful not to be caught riding through the judge's yard. There was no serious fighting, no profanity or meanness, just fun and games until dinner time each day of the summer. Some evenings we were allowed to "patrol" the neighborhood on our bikes as parents sat on the porch visiting with other neighbors.

High school and band trips, football and basketball games meant somewhere to go and it was not only essential but also our duty to support all school functions. Riding home on the bus from out of town games was a highlight for dating couples as they cuddled in the back seats. The rest of us tried to ignore what we imagined might be going on in the darkness while wondering if a certain boy or girl might possibly notice we were living and breathing.

There are faces of coaches, band directors, teachers, and fellow students that I visit when I time travel. I recall conversations and events with more clarity and meaning than they had at the time they were happening. The words of criticism shared by one person or another have become words of wisdom in my time traveling. The respect I gave teachers and gained by being a good student come back to me as words of encouragement over the years.

Frank Clark wrote: "Everyone is trying to accomplish something big, not realizing that life is made up of little things." Those time travels of your mind and heart are essential to your good health and happiness. They reward you over and over again with a feeling that your life has had meaning and purpose. If they do not, begin making memories today for travels tomorrow.

Peter Rabbit's Teeth

Once upon a time there was a youngster named Peter. He was just an ordinary young boy who loved getting dirty, could climb to the top of most trees, and could tantalize his sisters until they screamed to mom for help.

Peter lived on a farm and had certain chores he had to complete each day. In the winter he had to fetch firewood to the porch and clean out the mound of ashes in the fireplace. He and his sisters had to feed the chickens and make sure the cows had hay in their boxes and that all the other animals had their supper ready by nightfall.

Peter's favorite chore was seeing to his three rabbits. One rabbit was as white as the clouds and her pink ears seemed almost transparent. One rabbit was totally black except for a white spot just under his chin. His eyes were so dark they were hidden in the blackness of his fur.

Spot was the third bunny and Peter's favorite. He was white as snow except for a black circle that surrounded his left eye. The rabbits brought Peter lots of pleasure and he didn't even mind cleaning out their cages and the feeding chores each evening.

For several months the rabbits thrived under Peter's constant attention. They grew fat and fluffy and they bounded in the yard when Peter took them out of their cages. Two of the rabbits grew steadily but Spot seemed to decrease in size each day. He got skinnier and skinnier until Peter asked his dad what he should do.

Spot was placed in a separate cage because it appeared the other two rabbits were getting all the food

Peter was putting in the cage each night. Each day Peter rushed home to check on Spot in his new cage but the rabbit continued to lose weight. Even with the best carrots and the freshest lettuce, Spot would not eat.

Peter would sit and watch Spot as he sniffed, and pushed the food around in his cage. He seemed to want to eat but he did not take a bite of the vegetables. Peter finally discovered the reason for Spot's weight loss. His front teeth had grown so long he could not open his mouth wide enough to get the food in.

With his father's help, the front teeth were filed away and with this dental work complete, Spot could once again eat and grow fat. And this is a true story about a rabbit our sons had as children. It was a neat lesson for the family. We never dreamed teeth could grow too long to eat. Might be a good way to lose weight.

Made from Scratch

Have you ever heard the term "made from scratch"? Many years ago a friend told me she had been looking for Scratch in the grocery store. She was very serious with her remark. Being reared in the north, she had as many problems with grits, cracklin' cornbread, and hominy as we did keeping up with the speed of her vocabulary. Over the years, we adjusted to her speech speed and she has definitely learned about southern cooking.

"Scratch" means that you do not buy the cake in a box, do not buy a birthday card pre-printed, and do not buy clothes straight off the rack. What scratch means is that you make the items from start to finish with creativity, sewing, pasting, pinning, or measuring the ingredients listed in a recipe. It means slowing down our pace.

Elizabeth Berg wrote an article in Woman's Day several years ago entitled "What's Your Hurry?" My question is: "Do we ever have time for the cake to cool?" People are always in a hurry. They pass cars on yellow lines, in turning lanes, and blow their horns the minute a light turns green. They shift from foot to foot as they stand in line, blow and mumble, and often snarl when someone questions the cashier causing a delay of a few seconds.

People speed up to make it through caution lights, blink their lights at motorists in their way on 400 even though other cars are in their path, microwave minute rice, and do not wait for the beep on an answer machine. We rush home at night so we can get a bath and get in bed so we can get up in time to go to work so we can go home again. Most individuals spend their weekends trying to get a jump on the week ahead and are so geared up that

Saturdays and Sundays are neither days of leisure nor of rest.

My question is still the same: "Do we ever have time for the cake to cool?" In the "olden days" Mom would bake a cake, brownies, or some other treat from scratch, place it on a rack to cool, and the aroma of baking would permeate the house. The smell would entice children from play and Dads would just have to come in the house for a drink of water. In a few moments, a slow and unhurried family affair would take place around the kitchen table with cake, milk, brownies, or whatever Mom had cooked.

I am as guilty as the next person. I hurry to meet deadlines, complete tasks, and get in just one more job in the yard before dark befalls me. I grow impatient in lines, frown at motorists that do not know how to maneuver around the courthouse square, and rush from one place to another with my lists and errands to complete. But I often think about the time it took to bake the cake from scratch and to allow time for cooling before the icing was added. Perhaps we need to ask ourselves from time to time if it is necessary to go so fast and to do so much. Then maybe we would sit calmly for the ten minutes that "cooling" takes, doing nothing but enjoying the "aroma" of our life.

What will our generation be called?

According to Tom Brokaw, the name given to my generation is the Greatest Generation. In 1999, Brokaw wrote that people age 50 and beyond have been the movers, shakers, givers, and doers of the world. This generation has a reputation for having more moral standards, longer marriages, and more commitments to worthwhile endeavors. Of course, there are always exceptions to any given statement and people of every age can fall into the "Greatest" category.

I wonder how often we face the fact that some of the changes in society today are not for the best. When children are housed in day care centers five days a week, fathers and mothers work and travel to their jobs 40 to 50 miles away each day, and grandparents live in another state or around the world, how do we define "family"? When children expect rewards for good behavior and good grades, want exceptions to the rules for everyone else, and freedom from responsibilities, how do we define self discipline?

Does it disturb you that volunteers needed in churches, non-profit organizations, hospitals, Senior Centers, and service organizations are decreasing yearly and those that are giving of their time are retired and aging adults? Does it register with us at all that nowadays any work or time given must have monetary compensation? That the first and foremost question is "what does it pay?"

When we think over the last half of the 20th century we realize the impact of many aspects of education and family structure on American life styles. Mothers who do stay at home or home school their children are frowned upon because they do not have a job. Motherhood no longer holds the respect that it once enjoyed.

Education for everyone has produced competition between men and women for jobs and "bread winner" is difficult to define. More women in the work force makes for fewer women at home and depending on others to teach their children morals, manners, and rules of behavior.

The automobile has produced teenagers who have too much freedom, place too much burden on them and their family for insurance and car payments, and deprived them of a carefree youth because they must work to make money to go places.

The Greatest Generation had the responsibility of seeing to elderly parents, caring for and teaching their children right from wrong, fighting major wars and giving their lives for liberty and democracy. They were called upon over and over to make sacrifices, to give of their time to help others, defend their country, and share the responsibilities for a better world. Each generation might claim to be the greatest, but there will always be the question: "the greatest in what way"?

Non-violent ideal helped us survive

The first week of February 2006 began with the announcement of the death of Coretta Scott King. The same week, the President gave his State of the Union address, and Cindy Sheehan, again dishonoring the memory of her son who died in Iraq, was arrested in Washington. She stated she was arrested because she was wearing a shirt. Not wearing a shirt would have gotten her arrested, but wearing one?

The death of Mrs. King brought to mind an era remembered for its protests and civil rights movements. The death of Rosa Parks reminded us once again of the sacrifices and valiant stands made by many people at a time when the rights of all individuals were challenged.

Growing up during the 50's and 60's was often a time of fear and unease. Children were forced to attend schools in locations far from home and were bused to and from these schools, often under guards, so that equality could be attained. In small towns these situations brought out reasons for violence and cross burnings by adults in white robes with faces covered became commonplace once again.

Crowds of protestors became the lead story on the evening news every day. Church bombings killed innocent children in Sunday school. Sidewalks around schools were lined with police and national guardsmen and college campuses with flying bullets destroyed lives and families.

Young people were not only the focus of equal rights but they were the targets and often the recipients of the violence. Even though the term "non-violence" became the focus of each movement, all along the sidelines of the movement individual families were targeted and often members were killed.

Remembering those times and having watched the history channel films of that period of time has enlightened many people. It seemed that there was no unrest in my town, however, there were certainly other towns where the focus of violence was a constant fear. Women and children huddled in cellars and behind closed doors while strangers threatened them.

We do not like to dwell on those issues of the past. We like to sugar coat the roles of people we knew who were upstanding individuals by daylight and monsters after the sun went down. We like to say we were never against equal rights and even now we may hesitate to afford equality to everyone.

Over the last 50 years progress has been made in human rights. However, equal opportunities no matter what race, color, national origin or sex has not become the priority of all Americans. We can look back to the time when these rights were not available to everyone and be grateful that the movement leaders were insistent upon non-violence. Even though their idea was often ignored, just think what could have happened if this had not been the focus?

The "N" Word

I don't like to use the "N" word but there are a lot of them running around loose. There is the nut driving down the road at 60 miles per hour with less than a car length between his front bumper and my back one. There is the nut behind the wheel of a fast automobile dipping in and out of three or more lanes of traffic pretending he is at the Indy 500 race but is definitely endangering everyone's life on the road.

The person who thinks he cannot have an accident or cause one by driving reckless is a classic example of what we older people refer to as a "Nut" so hard headed that smart cannot escape, and who has a definite need to be cracked, punched, chopped, or kept in a shell for safety's sake. Before you drive around the courthouse one time or try to maneuver around the shopping centers any time of the day, you can probably call several people the "N" word.

There are many people out in public who venture in and out of stores on an hourly basis who could be labeled with the "N" word. There is the shopper who leaves the shopping cart in the middle of the aisle while browsing two aisles away. There is the person who knocks the merchandise off the pegs and steps over it without reaching down to pick it up.

There is the one who leaves a cart in the parking spaces instead of taking three steps to place it in the rack. But the worst one is the uncaring individual who makes unkind remarks to employees and uses profanity by the "mouthful".

There are the folks who blow horns the instant the light changes color. There are people who believe that rules were made for everyone except them and promptly ignore: "Keep Off the Grass, Keep Right, Do Not Disturb, Handicapped Parking, Senior Citizens Only". There are the N's who break in front of the lines, walk around people waiting for the next bathroom stall, and push ahead of people at restaurant counters. Nuts, nerds, not nice, nasty manners, nefarious (detestable), nervy, nitwit, noisome (disgusting), nonessential, and the list of "n" words could go on and on.

We make such a "to do" about the least little thing these days. We make an issue out of the use of a word that heretofore had not been so important but now we must be politically correct. The media has so captured the minds of people that talk shows advertise for the nuts and nerds of society to speak up, speak out, and tell all their sordid and sexual absurdities.

We allow the nuts and nerds of the world to decide that we like child pornography advertising jeans, we like to hear profanity on cartoon shows and stupidity is acceptable for first-rate audience appeal programming. Ridiculous isn't it?

You may recall the time when you heard the phrase, "The nerve of that person!" You may even remember the time when there were a few eccentrics in each community but they didn't cause much trouble. There was the goat man, the fellow who lived in the shack outside town and wore strange clothes, and the old lady who lived in the scary house with the shades always pulled down.

These were the strange and unusual people we knew and now we are considered strange and unusual if we use good sense, have nice manners, and don't air our "dirty laundry" in public. And, if you have a good dictionary you can find many other words that are just as strong and just as politically incorrect as the "N" word.

Heritage of the Young

In 1976 an executive decision was made by the giant television networks to lower the barriers on what could and could not be shown on television. They allowed a bit of profanity, a scene or two of partially clothed people, and one or two "bed scenes". And then they waited for a public outcry against the indecency. They waited and they waited, and none came.

The barriers, once lowered for a test of decency and morality for the media, was a "go ahead" for what we now have. The language and the scenes that were once slightly risqué are now appalling on many programs. We not only have these aspects of what is entertainment, but also we have all of the family skeletons out of closets and all the dirty laundry displayed at prime time.

The American people have, again and again failed to stand up and be counted. When atheist Madelyn Murray O'Hare started her quest of eliminating any prayer or Bible reading in schools, people kept their seats. Beginning in 1960 she filed against the Baltimore School District and the results were nation wide when the Supreme Court ruled in her favor.

These are big changes that we have witnessed over the decades in the morals and ethics categories. We have watched the dress code of teenagers to sink below the waistline until some are embarrassingly close to being indecent. With the availability of tattoos we are now accosted with the artwork on every conceivable place that a person can display it on their bodies.

From the above paragraphs you might think I'm against television, the Supreme Court, tattoos and teenagers. That is not true. I am against being complacent with changes that are made bit by bit without any notice until they become acceptable and unmanageable. Okay, what do I mean?

First of all we are at a point in our history when it seems nothing is taboo and anything is permissible. The vile, the violence, the improper and immoral behavior of celebrities are touted on tabloids, as "entertainment", and as acceptable. The psychics are controlling the information shows and even the animals must now be analyzed for their behavior.

As long as the public is quietly accepting of these changes, they will continue to degrade and demoralize the fabric of America. The backbone of America supposedly has always been the family but with the divorce rate in America exceeding all other industrialized countries that statement is unraveling too.

We lived much of this History

Who was Jack Ruby? What year did the first astronaut leave an orbiting spacecraft? When did the first man walk on the moon and who was he? Who set the record for pitching four no-hitters in a row? When was the first test tube baby born, and where? Can you answer these questions?

Students have always had a hard time accepting the fact that many useless items of information are stored in their brain and will never be used: a pie being square, a predicate is a verb, who was Winston Churchill, Walt Whitman, or Dwight Eisenhower. What is what and who is who in the world outside the perimeter of entertainment does not seem to be very important. Having the latest CD, seeing a movie before it has been released over a week, keeping up with Bart Simpson and South Park kids, latest styles, these are the priorities.

Could you believe parents and students complaining because the student did not pass the "test" and would not graduate from high school? There must be a misunderstanding somewhere along the line that allows students to believe that test results and passing grades do not in any way determine their eligibility to graduate. However, I am bewildered by the fact that students who did not pass the test and did not graduate were eligible for the Hope Scholarship.

Update the curriculum! First it was reading, then math, then science. Add to that curriculum Military Strategy for playground, lunchroom, and hallways. While the curriculum plans are being made for schools, both private and public, consider a course designed to instill in youngsters the fact that life is hard, dangerous at times, unhappiness is inevitable during certain periods, nothing is obtained legally without work and effort, and stealing and killing are against the law.

We may have forgotten in our pursuit of educational standards those facts that should be common knowledge. The average teenager may know the top 10 rap and rock records, how to program a VCR, how to surf the internet to find the latest porno pictures, but may be clueless about sound waves, rhythm and musical signs, or scientific knowledge concerning tobacco products.

Perhaps many facts we learned in the 60's and 70's were useless. It may not matter that Jack Ruby killed Lee Harvey Oswald who killed President John Kennedy. It may not be necessary to know Aleksei A. Leonov was the first to leave an orbiting spacecraft in 1965, or that Neil Armstrong was first and Edwin E. Aldrin was second to walk on the moon in 1968. Unless you will be on Jeopardy, knowing that Sandy Koufax pitched the four no-hitters and the first test tube baby was born in London in 1978 may take up lots of brain space.

Curiosity and knowledge are of vital importance. As we learn, we grow; as we explore and become knowledgeable in many areas we become better citizens.

What is good education?

At the age of ten, Virginia Cary Hudson wrote a delightful book entitled, "O Ye Jigs and Juleps". Well over a million copies of this little book have been sold and are so wonderfully childlike and truthful it is worth reading and sharing.

Virginia states that education is "what you learn in books, and nobody knows you know it but your teacher". She asked her friend Mrs. Harris what good Marco Polo would ever do her and Mrs. Harris said education gave you satisfaction. Virginia thought that she would rather be ignorant and have fun than be educated and have satisfaction.

There is a great deal of truth in the fact that education brings you satisfaction but it is also true there is a lot of education you never use. For example, I've never used algebra, chemistry formulas, some science facts and a lot of geography. Even the names of countries I once knew are no longer on maps. Of course, the rules of English still apply, but editing has put aside most of them as being burdensome.

Many facts and figures that use to take up space in my brain have now decayed or been lost somewhere between my ears in the parts of my brain no longer operating. Those senior moments or whatever the newest catch phrase happens to be, attack older and younger adults without discrimination and can wreak havoc with our comfort levels.

Virginia and her friend Mrs. Harris, who remained young at heart, traveled along the road of childhood together. Mrs. Harris was responsible for many learning experiences about gardening, proper manners, personal appearance, and giving parties. She was a role model for Virginia, teaching her and taking the time to explain how and why things were done in a certain way.

In our society neighbors are mostly unknown and older people are often thought to be a nuisance rather than a good example. Young children are forever missing opportunities to learn how to plant a garden, pick the right beans, plant bulbs and pull weeds. These may seem trivial, but the conversations that can take place in a garden cannot be labeled as trivial.

Virginia wrote, "Mrs. Harris plays the piano for me. She taught me to pick the young beans instead of the old ones. She taught me how to churn. Mrs. Harris takes me fishing and I carry the worms and the lunch, but not in the same box. Mrs. Harris is cute and when she dies I am going to cry and cry."

There are so many older people in my memory that gave me precious moments of time, their energy and instructions. Those lessons I learned as a youngster from older special friends have stayed with me more than algebra and geography. Virginia's book reminded me of their "lessons for life".

One of these days

In 1966 Ann Landers reprinted a letter she had used many years before. The letter, written by a grown child concerned her "busyness". Each time she visited with her mother she had failed to spend time with her. She always had too many things to do until the year when she could no longer sit down for a visit with her mom.

It is entirely too often that I hear myself and others say these four words: "One of these days". Too often I watch as one of those days turns into no more days. A phone call, or an unexpected drop by visit to an older person are more than appreciated, they are lifesavers. Taking a few minutes, freely given and well spent can make our day worthwhile. Because we are in too big of a hurry, we miss many opportunities to make a difference.

"One of these days", I am going to stop procrastinating and clean out that closet. One of these days I am going to organize all those pictures into albums. One of these days I am going to sit down and read a good book. One of these days we will take that trip we have been promising ourselves.

One of these days I am going to visit my aunt who lives only an hour away. One of these days I am going to send a picture of the grandchildren to her. One of these days I am going to do something different with my time and do one of those items I keep putting off until a better time.

Why don't I call my friend and say, "Let's do lunch"? Why don't I drop by the retirement home and see how another friend is doing? Why have I not sent that note of sympathy? Why have I not gotten that wedding present?

Why have I not bought a present for that new baby who will soon be a year old?

Why are we always too busy? We can keep asking ourselves the same question over and over again. What is so important that putting off until a better time becomes easy for us? Why are a few errands more important than five minutes on the phone with a special friend? Why are our schedules so crowded that a 15-minute visit is prohibitive?

As I read the column from Ann Landers I was once again reminded about how fragile and unpredictable time is. I was reminded again about the lack of opportunities to fulfill those promises of "one of these days".

Are Boys Different?

Are boys different? You better believe it! It is often a mind-altering discovery for adults who are seldom around young children. For those teachers and parents of both boys and girls this is a known fact.

We always enjoy having our nephew in our house. He is very active and filled with immeasurable excitement. Even the "man of the house" had forgotten how aggressive, energetic, and enthusiastic a young boy can be. After a few hours he begins to remember days gone by when our sons were just as vibrant, busy, and into everything possible.

I am often prompted to reread several chapters of Dr. James Dobson's book "Bringing Up Boys". I find many passages that are familiar. One written by Plato 2300 years ago: "Of all the animals, the boy is the most unmanageable."

"Mother use to say" is now commonplace in my vocabulary. She would say" boys will be boys" or, "that is what boys do!" All of the answers didn't fit, as I would lament my futile attempt to make our boys sit quietly through just one meal. As they snickered and squirmed their way around the food they didn't like I bemoaned the fact that they would soon die of starvation. They didn't!

Boys are quite different than a little girl who will sit in a restaurant and not want to see what is over the booth wall and converse with the other patrons. The young girl will talk with her doll and cuddle it to her breast as the little boy runs his car along the railing between the booths and ask the man if he has a truck. .

Boys have three questions to answer where toys are concerned. Will it come apart? Will it make noise? What makes it work? Once these questions are explored he will move on to the next exciting adventure of getting in the dog crate with the dog captured inside with him.

Boys can disappear and can remain quieter than a mouse as adults go wild looking in all nooks and crannies for them. They are amazed when found that the adults are angry instead of laughing joyously because the lost one has been found.

In distinguishing the difference between boys and girls one should keep in mind that boys are much more curious about handles, machinery, and engines of all kinds. They want to see how much water will come out of a faucet, how many times a commode can be flushed without breaking the handle, and how many times they can pull a mower string before they are exhausted.

Little boys have heroes. They are not obsessive, only possessive. They want all the ninja turtle figures, all the power rangers, and all of the paraphernalia that goes with them. Once the collection is complete they will move on to another hero figure.

Dobson writes: "So buckle your seat belts! There are a lot of interesting grounds you will cover with boys." Enjoy the ride. I did!

Riding the School Bus

He hesitated slightly as the doors opened on the bus. A backward glance towards his mother meant that in a moment the doors would close behind him and he would be off to another world where she could only visit on special occasions. Reluctantly he stepped forward peering upward into a giant hole and saw the smile on a face he did not know. "Come on son," the friendly driver said, "we are running late!"

The laughter coming from inside the bus was loud and his throat began to close up as he climbed the steps and looked for a place to sit. So many children of all ages and he was surely the smallest one on the bus. All those happy tunes about the wheels on the bus and the people on the bus didn't make him feel one bit better this first morning of school.

He walked slowly to the back searching for a seat until finally he reached an empty place. There was a big guy sitting by the window and he slid in beside him. The face looked familiar but the small boy did not know why. The older boy called him by name and said, "sit by me and I'll make sure no one bothers you." Perhaps the first day wouldn't be too bad the child thought.

Round and round the neighborhood and through strange places the bus rolled until finally he could see the school. His friend told him what to do when he got off the bus and as he walked slowly down the aisle his friend called to him, "I'll see you this afternoon. Have fun!" Down at the bottom of the steps was the smiling face of the lady mom said was his teacher. He felt safer now that he saw a familiar face.

But then a crowd began to gather around her and there was shouting, crying, and pushing. He wasn't use to this and that same lump began to creep back into his throat. Tears were just behind his eyes but he forced them back. He wasn't sure he liked this new world and he was positive he missed his mom and the security of knowing she was just in the other room. It was such a big place when you didn't have your mom or dad by the hand.

The hall was long and there were many turns before he entered a bright and beautiful classroom. There were fun things on the walls and books everywhere. He had his own desk and a place for his new Star Wars notebook and his sharp pencil. His teacher was so nice and when the children quit crying the morning was over in a hurry and it was time for lunch.

The cafeteria was loud and there were lots of kids everywhere carrying trays and he wasn't sure he could handle something like that without dropping it. But he managed to get to a table and the food wasn't as good as mom's, but it was okay. He could make it till he could get home for the special treat his mom promised.

Before long it was time to go home and he followed his teacher eagerly as she "found" the front door and his bus was there. His friend called to him as he walked towards the back of the bus and patted the seat beside him. "How was your day," he asked. "I'm glad it is over, but I'll probably go back again tomorrow." And with that, he sat down for the short ride home.

He was too little to go to school!

When school begins each year, it matters not if you have a child beginning his or her first day of school, your mind will still rush back to the first day of school for your own children.

With a rush, I recalled how I had mixed emotions as I slowly drove our son Will to his first day of school. With a brave smile and a positive attitude I babbled on about what fun he would have, how nice the teacher would be, and how many friends he would make. I remember now how small his hand felt in my hand and how he looked up at me with the question written all over his face, "Do we have to go in there?"

He held my hand tightly and tried to be a big boy, but I could tell he was also trying to hold back the time when he would have to turn loose and go his own way into a strange world filled with new adventures. I can remember a feeling of anger that I had against all those people who thought that the education of "my child" should begin at age five. How had "they" come to the terrible conclusion that my "baby" was ready for school?

He was just a little fellow with his book bag, his new pencils, his new clothes and shoes. How could complete strangers know if he was big enough to take on the whole world? As we wound through the building, down halls, pass noisy classrooms with other children and parents pushing their way to other rooms, I can still see the apprehension on the face of my child, and every other child heading towards that" unknown adventure".

I can still remember the look that was on my face as well as the look on the faces of other mothers as we held our child's hand; the look said that time from birth to first grade had been too short. And I knew with that walk down the hall we would both rush rapidly through childhood. In a moments time both of our children would be in school, graduate from high school, complete college, and have many events in-between that would be so quick that they would be a blur for me.

A child is someone who passes through our life and then disappears into an adult. We are wise if we take every opportunity to enjoy our children, sacrifice a few luxuries to spend time with them instead of money on them, let the work wait sometime so that we can listen to their problems instead of thinking about our own, and know that those precious years will pass by much faster than we want them to pass.

He left home a child

August always seems to be a month of happenings, especially among our family and friends. There are major birthdays, exciting anniversaries, senior school years, and off to college or the business world. It is always a month of remembering for parents with the transitions of life and the beginning of another school year.

He was so small as he lugged the book bag up the steps filled with his assortment of supplies. He was both scared and excited for his first day at school. He wanted to go on this new adventure but was not quite ready to turn loose of the security of his mom's hand.

I was skeptical about letting my child fend for himself in the big, big world of school. As I led him into the building and let go of his hand I suddenly had the urge to call out to him: "Please don't be old enough to leave me. I'm not quite through having you under foot asking questions. I haven't had quite enough time to get accustomed to letting you grow up!"

His little blonde head melted among the heads of other children as he raced toward this new adventure. Suddenly I realized he had stepped into another world of changing and growing, one that would last a while and change into yet another bigger and wider world. These would be worlds where I would not always be and as the changes occurred he would grow more and more independent.

He was happy with his new friends and excited about being one of the gang. He loved his teacher and had already found his seat and was checking in with the boys and girls he knew. He would not turn around and watch me trying to hide tears and pad slowing out of his new world. As I strolled slowly back to my car, I glanced back several times expecting to see him running to catch up with me. He didn't!

My thoughts immediately changed both times as I walked our sons to their first day of school. I had always known they were safe, or if they were doing something dangerous or harmful. Now I had to trust others for this care. I had to release them to the world of bullies, bad talk, and pressure from his peers.

I lingered a few extra minutes in the parking lot with other mothers. I hoped that I had equipped our sons for their lifelong journey. I hoped we had made them strong enough to resist wrong choices and to express their opinions about right and wrong. I hope they carried with them the respect for themselves, their friends and their teachers. I knew they had good manners and they knew how to behave; I hoped they practiced these every day.

Housework Will Wait

She is only three years old but a set of earrings, necklace, and bracelet from The Dollar Store makes her eyes sparkle. She dons her jewelry, cradles the doll in her arms, smoothing the blanket around the feet and rocks back and forth until she is assured the baby is asleep. She gently places her in the bed, and quietly she goes about her work in the kitchen preparing the pretend meal for her family. She begins mixing and pouring until she has the cake just right for the oven, constantly checking on the items in the various pots on the stove.

His mother watches as he bounces up the driveway in his best shoes stomping through the mud holes left in the driveway from last night's rain. The mud splatters onto his jeans, and she cringes at the thought of her chore of getting out the mud and grass stains once again.

He seems delighted as he watches the brown water bounce around his feet. Then he revves up his pretend motorcycle and roars through the house swaying first one way and then the other as he dodges between the chairs with a near miss of lamps and causing the glass objects to teeter on their perch. He is only five but his imagination is already in full swing as he grabs a black cloth and begins constructing his pirate costume.

She climbs up in her mother's lap with her book, eager for story time. The fragrance from the soap and toothpaste will linger with her mom long after the story is complete. In a moment her older brother snuggles under mom's other arm ready for their usual quiet time before bed. Dad is late and Mom is the substitute reader for tonight, and before the story begins the question is asked: "Will Dad be home before we have to go to bed?"

Life might not have been this easy for most of us growing up. Long term memories may be of the financial stains of depression years, fathers gone to war, hard work from dawn till dusk on farms, the hand-me-down clothes from child to child to child, and the meager portions of toys and games of childhood, all of which may lead some to believe that children have it too easy these days.

We love to reminisce and we are constantly reminded of the challenges to our own imagination as we sought out the ways to entertain ourselves as children. A best-dressed lady might don a hat of moss, a necklace strung from clover and mix mud pies in a jar lid.

A young man might spend hours sweeping and moving pine needles for his fort or dig holes in hard Georgia clay to make pathways and roads for his little cars made from scrapes of wood. Older youngsters would venture further than the edge of the yard and skinny dip in the creek in the summertime heat or search for crawdads along the banks.

The sights and sounds of childhood linger with parents and children. The constant and endless supply of dirty clothes to wash, the homework chores, the baths and stories, and the games of pretend stimulate our memories and offer warmth to our hearts. We delight in telling our children and grandchildren we walked two miles to school carrying a pail of cold biscuits with jelly. We emphasize the hardships of not having anyone to pick us up from school and having to make that thirty minute bus trip home each day.

As a young mother I learned a very valuable lesson about rearing children. The lesson was a simple one and has been used by me over and over again with young mothers. The lesson, "Housework will wait, growing children will not!"

Homework Can Wait

Toys were scattered about the room and any visitor to our house had to step over them if they did not "call ahead'. If they called I would work diligently to make a path to a sofa or a chair. It is somewhat similar these days. My nephew Jacob and I are seriously into building Lego structures on the coffee table in the living room.

I always enjoyed the "moments" of our boys growing up. Folding clothes or mopping a floor could be done after they were in bed. The floors had to be mopped on a regular basis or the health Department might condemn our house. Folding clothes happened when there was no more underwear in their drawers.

Housework was always done around two energetic boys. I never remember competing a task without stopping a dozen times to answer a question or referee a scuffle. There were very few meals cooked without turning off the stove at least once for an emergency of one kind or another.

With growing children there were always spills, house cleaning, washing, folding clothes, and starting over immediately after finishing one job and doing it again. There was never a bath time when the floor was not wet along with the boys, and never one for me that a dozen questions didn't puncture my relaxed atmosphere. Always this one, "How much longer will you be?"

Our boys grew up too fast and now I have plenty of time to dust furniture or mop floors. However, I now have another problem. These chores don't seem so important anymore. The furniture may look a little rough, the sofa and chairs aren't perfect, but they are presentable to visitors.

There are moments when I try very hard to see those two little boys scuffling on the floor or laying on their stomachs watching cartoons. There are sights and sounds I miss like a good yell, "Mother make him give that back to me!" I enjoyed their differences, the notebooks filled with art instead of math. The 15 minutes of piano practice punctuated by another 10 without a note played.

For those who wonder where the days go and about the number of chores undone and no energy to do any more, let me assure you that a little dirt never hinder the growth of children. A lot of dirt will cause problems, but dusty furniture doesn't. Floors will always need cleaning, and clothes will always need washing and folding. There will always be dishes to put up and more will be left in the sink.

What clever ways we have of reminding ourselves, our children, and grandchildren that these are the "best of times and the worst of times", and our memories are still an opportunity to relive those happy childhood experiences.

For sure, our children will not be around forever for picnics, play time, story time, nor will they always be available for conversations, they grow up!

How can you tell the good guys?

"I don't like the bad guys. I just like the good guys." This from a six year old who was choosing which of the actions figures he would like to have. I asked how he could tell the good guys from the bad guys and he said, "you just know!"

As children, we played cowboys and Indians and sometimes I was a cowgirl and more often I had to be the Indian. In our childhood the Indian was always defeated. Then we played war games and dug foxholes and shot the enemies and bad guys from the protection of the dirt. Mother was always wary of the challenges of washdays after war episodes.

Years later our sons donned the capes of the heroes of the day. There were Batman, Robin, Superman, and yes, even Spiderman. There were good guys and bad guys and but the good ones always had special outfits to go along with their abilities. Some of the characters of 30 plus years ago are still fighting the bad guys today.

I read the Devinci Code, some of the Harry Potter books, and even read several of the C.S. Lewis books about Narnia. I have seen the movies except for the Code. With my nephew I have watched all the episodes of Star Wars and we watch many fights of the Power Rangers on television as they defeat the evil creatures.

I can understand how many parents fear their child watching some of these movies or reading some of these books. I can understand how children who aren't quite sure about the difference in right and wrong could be confused with these characters. If these same children live in an environment that does not include the teachings of living right and not doing harm to their friends and neighbors, I can understand their parents defending their undeveloped minds.

However, when a young child, living in an atmosphere of loving instruction of right and wrong, can identify the good guys from the bad ones, what is the problem? In watching the movie, Narnia, the bad guys were horrid looking while the good guys, even the lion, had a look of kindness about them. The lesson from that movie was distinct. Evil looks and acts bad. Perhaps, children know more than we suspect.

When parents try to ban books or control all sorts of actions and reactions in schools concerning literature, I want to ask other questions. Do we recognize the bad guys from the good guys? Have we kept the bad guys out of the classrooms and from harming our children? Have we taught our children to avoid situations that are wrong and could be harmful? Do we know about the sites they visit on the Internet?

There are many good lessons to be learned from some of these books. Parents might try reading a few of them. Better still, discuss them with your child.   And take the time to enjoy their lives while they still want you to watch them.

Wait just a minute!

He could hear the drone of the machinery through the halls, across the driveway, and up the hill. He knew there were backhoes, dump trucks, and earth movers busy on the other end of the building. His eyes sparkled with the anticipation of seeing these huge machines in action and his teacher had to say more than once, "Not now, Zachary, we will go later!"

There were dresses of every color and description hung on the racks. She skipped from outfit to outfit and her dancing eyes revealed she had found the perfect outfit. Then, she spotted another one, and another that were also perfect. As mom watched her child's excitement, she had to say over and over again, "We cannot buy them all!"

He really didn't want his mom and dad to know that he would be disappointed if they did not make the meeting so he did not make a big deal out of the occasion. He was a big boy now and he rarely asked them to attend school functions because they were busy with their jobs and he knew they probably could not make it home on time for his special night. His name was called and he stepped forward to receive the award. As he turned he spotted his parents at the back of the room and his face shone with excitement.

The first homerun, and Dad is not here to see it! That first pair of high heels, only two inches, but Mom didn't help pick them out! She gets a good citizen award and no one is there to witness the occasion. Important times in the life of a child, but how often do we as parents miss the excitement of the little boys and girls we call our children?

How often do we think, or don't think? Sure, the story time is good, but we don't have time to do our job much less read a story to our children? How many of us feel guilty because the band plays every ballgame and we've heard them before but this is the first one for our child and we are not there? How often do we put our obligations to other people and other situations before those to our children?

As we see our little boys become big men and our little girls become women, will we look back over the years of their childhood with regrets or with countless memories we have made with them? Will the children of parents who are labeled Generation X, whose lives are filled with obligations and deadlines, careers and abundant demands for excellence, comparative homes, jobs, and assets; will this generation know the true joy of what makes little girls and boys special and what is of major importance to them at the different ages and stages of their lives?

Remember this: "What are little boys made out of? Snakes and snails, and puppy dog tails, that's what little boys are made out of ! What are little girls made out of? Sugar and spice and everything nice, that's what little girls are made out of !" And this nursery tale: "Hey, diddle diddle, the cat and the fiddle; the cow jumped over the moon. The little boy laughed to see such fun and the dish ran away with the spoon." Do you hear the giggles of your children as you read these rhymes?

Once Upon A Time

Once upon a time there was a little girl who lived in a very small town. She knew her next-door neighbors and she could always find at their house a glass of water on a hot day and something warm on a cold day. Her parents did not worry about her when she visited next door because the people were just like them; they loved children and treated them with kindness. They even expected her to behave in their house.

The little girl went to school just up the street. She knew all the teachers in her school by name and they knew her name and who her parents were and where she lived. One rainy day when she forgot her umbrella her teacher even took her home so she would not get wet. In her school were other children who lived on her street and just around the corner from her house. School was fun and she could not wait to go each day.

Holidays were special and birthdays; they were the grandest times in the year. Her mom would bake a caramel cake, the best she ever ate and the candles multiplied each year, but she could still blow them out on the first try. Of course there would be presents, besides Christmas this was the only other special time when presents were given to her. The wrapping was always pretty and there was usually some item or another that she had wished for long and hard.

When it snowed the little girl would bundle up in every piece of clothes she could get on her body. She would hurry out to help other children make snowballs and snowmen, and her hands would turn blue from the cold, but she wasn't really cold she would tell her mom. Snow ice cream would be the treat of the day followed closely by the hot chocolate made on the stove from cocoa, milk, sugar, and some magical ingredient that made it just right for little cold bodies.

On summer days when the sun was so hot adults sat on the porch with a fan, the little girl and her friends would run merrily through the sprinkler until the yard was soaked and soggy. There was not much crying except of course when someone was hurt or when the bigger kids tried to change the rules and wouldn't play fair, but that wasn't a very big deal when an adult said behave or you will have to come in the house.

Once upon a time when the little girl grew up and had children of her own she looked around for a small town just like she had lived in as a child. She searched everywhere and could not find a place exactly like she remembered her hometown. After much searching she choose a town that gave her glimpses of her childhood days, a community with streets and sidewalks and lights around the town.

"Once upon a time" begins many stories for children but just as important are the once upon a time stories of adults. They are filled with the remember when's of old friends and the I recall's of conversations with new friends. They are the fabric and fiber of our heritage and they are nestled snugly in the security of our memories.

Helpful Sibling Advice

I was in the toy department, a place that I often visit for a small surprise for one child or another when I heard two young boys talking. I stopped and eavesdropped on their conversation. "The older boy told his younger brother, "No, that costs too much for Mom, we have to wait for Santa Claus to bring that one."

The youngsters moved from toy to toy examining the prices on the toys and with each selection the older child would tell the younger one if it was for the Santa list or if it might be one Mom would consider that day.

I was impressed by the attention this older sibling gave to his little brother. His patience and his care in explaining to him the logic of waiting for Santa's list was a clear indication of his exceptional maturity.

Now, these boys were perhaps four and eight years old. Their Mom was a short distance away, but I could tell the rules of being careful in stores had not been lost on the boys. The older child would remark to the younger one, "don't touch, that might break!" He would carefully replace the item his brother had picked up.

Toy departments in most stores are designed so that most children can observe the latest in engineering and advertising products. The characters from their favorite television cartoons are available on everything from washcloths and underwear to toothbrushes and lunch boxes. The array of items available for their selections was endless.

As a child we did not go to the stores for Christmas shopping. We did not get to browse the aisles in the local toy departments to select a new toy each time we visited. Our toy boxes were either discarded shoeboxes or would be in a small container because new shoes weren't purchased often.

When Christmas rolled around each year the toys we had were so worn and battered anything we received was a treat. The arrival of the Sears' Wish Book around the first of November was as exciting as the arrival of the tooth fairy or the Easter bunny.

The arrival of the Wish Book was an exciting adventure for us. After we had finished our daily chores we could curl up with the book in a big chair or on the sofa, if we could get along with each other. We scanned each page for our selections for Santa and if we were really good, we might get some of our choices under the tree.

For two months, the excitement grew, and grew until we could hardly contain ourselves. Our toys had not accumulated all year and our parents did not have to cull them to make room for the new ones.

Children still get excited over Christmas and I have to share blame for over-indulging even our grown children during the year. I will admit, waiting for Christmas has always been a big problem for me. It is even now.

Boys will be boys!

He comes into the house and in a short time he has a new fort made out of the cushions from the sofa and chairs. His Mom, like me, knows it is a boy thing and that a few misplaced cushions on the floor and the fun he is having will equal out in the long run. It is a boy thing!

A garden hose and a mud puddle are boy things too. Walking around a puddle is a girl thing and marching triumphantly across a puddle is a boy thing. Filling up your shoes and putting Power Rangers to sail in them across a mud puddle is also a boy thing. Looking appalled at the spectacle is a girl thing.

Lori Borgman in a 2005 commentary wrote: "Parents take note: Boys aren't showing up on the radar screen like they used to, little boys, big boys, high school and even college boys."

In five short years, research from the U.S. Department of Education projected that females would compose 60% of the national student body. Females already graduate at a higher rate than males and the math skills are rapidly becoming female dominated.

What is happening to our male children? John Rosemond, a noted speaker and child psychologist, thinks that we are trying to make boys more girl like. We want them to sit still and be quiet. Instructors believe boys are trouble and girls are well behaved. Of course, the recent shootings by male students and the acts of violence by men gives us pause to ponder all aspects of child rearing.

Borgman wrote: "Ask any mother who has raised both sexes. She may not be able to tell you which is easier, but she will tell you that they are markedly different." Boys do not need to be rescued from themselves as much as we need to recognize that they are different and provide different methods of teaching them to overcome their tendencies to fight their way through the world.

Women have come a long way in the world since the 70's and 80's. Equal employment opportunities and pay equal to men for the same job are expected in the work place. After men compete daily in the work places for superiority are they turning to violence and rage to get their way at home?

The phrase "you go girl" has taken females to a higher plateau and happily that has been the case. Females now constitute the majority of the applicants to medical and law schools. But what happened to the boys?

This question has been asked so many times by school administrators and the judicial systems that First Lady Laura Bush highlighted programs for boys during the president's second term.

"Boys will be boys," is not just a catch phrase to excuse their behavior. It is a way that we must look at our young boys and decide what needs to be done to make them into responsible adults. How do we teach them self-control and respect for themselves and others when they see men beating women, molesting children, and killing their classmates?

Halloween Pranks

Once upon a time, the beginning of October was the time to prepare for the fun of Halloween. Kids would start hoarding the toilet paper and the shaving soap and all the other paraphernalia for the harmless pranks of October. Now, they must be very careful to avoid being arrested for their Halloween joy.

There are so many tales of fun and games that we could recite. Painting the big windows on stores in town was harmless and it meant that one time during the year the merchants would have clean windows for their stores. All that shaving cream and tempera paint seemed to mix well to dissolve the filth from the glass.

There were always treks to neighbors to move the porch furniture to someone else's house. The result was in order to locate your property; you took a stroll around the neighborhood to talk with your neighbors asking about your furniture. It might be a good idea in this day and time to have an opportunity to speak to your neighbors.

There were always the annual removals of the outhouse belonging to one man down the road and "borrowing" another man's trailer to make the trip easier. We worked hard to do this in one night and not get caught by the ever-resourceful deputies. Of course, it always wound up on top of a building in downtown the following morning.

On many occasions, one person or another caught us. Of course, our parents were called to come and retrieve their notorious kids. There was punishment you can be sure and it was not a mere "grounding" time period. Looking back now, the punishments were not so harsh because the pranks were expected and tolerated by most adults.

I believe these activities had a positive effect on us kids. We knew we would more than likely get caught for some of these activities and escape capture for others. We knew the results of our fun might mean cleaning up the yard we had rolled. There were times we had to apologize to someone we thought was an old grouch, that's why he was selected for the "roll" experience. Never the less, it was not too painful.

We were good kids all year long and our pranks were harmless fun. We accepted the punishment as part of the procedure and vowed we would be more careful the next year. Careful, that is, and not be careless and get caught again.

This one night a year kept us good all year long. We learned stealth, ingenuity, and the purpose of a master plan. We were challenged to succeed and we were aware of the consequences. What other experience can teach a youngster all of these principles? Just kidding!!!

Children do grow up

In 1978 and article was written by Carole Klein in McCall's magazine entitled, "The Myth of the Perfect Parent". In 1995, Sue Browder wrote an article entitled, "Raising a G rated child in an X rated world."

What a difference a few years make! In 1978 parents were concerned with rearing a perfect child. The fact that a teacher would say a child did not seem happy at times could devastate a parent. While a parent would rarely assume responsibility for a child's cold or skinned knees, they often blamed themselves for the emotions, the wrong choices made by their teenagers, and the fact that their youngster was not as smart, not as popular, or could not handle stress like other children did.

The realization that we greatly influence our children's personalities has too often led to the belief that we carry full responsibility for every aspect of their emotional health and their behavior. In Cambridge, Mass. a 15 year old "child' was arraigned for murder. His friends were appalled because the bail was too high. They could not understand the "big deal" because people die every day.

Today, abstinence and chastity are unknown words even to young adults. The prospect of contracting a disease that can be fatal is only now beginning to sink into the general population of young people and adults as well. We have a nation that considers nude, crude, and rude as a way of life and acceptable even in our own living rooms.

We have moved from what Carole Klein wrote in 1978 about childhood being a special time of life when the most important two people in a child's life was their parents to the most important people in a child's life may be rock or movie stars, daycare workers, a good school teacher, or maybe even a bad one. We have changed from parents having conferences with teachers to calling on a phone and talking to computers. We have gone from housewives and homemakers to nannies, grannies, and home alone kids.

I am sure there are exceptions to these general statements. There are some families that believe that Mom caring for children is an honorable profession even for an educated person. There are some Dads who believe that spending time with his children is just as important as spending time with his friends. Thetre are some children who anticipate and look forward to sharing their day's work with both parents around a dinner table. And this may be a rarity.

When it comes to teaching moral and ethical behavior, we as parents must take full responsibility. We must teach our children right from wrong and not expect the public schools to do the job for us. We must take the responsibility for discipline instead of letting our children dictate our behavior and tell us what to do. When a three year old controls adults there is definitely a problem.

Sometimes, I believe that we forget that the way to rear children is to let them see us do the right thing and imitate our behavior. Sue Browder says that children often follow the footsteps that his parents thought they had covered up. She may be right!

What is Worthwhile?

Jacob was sitting in the back seat as we hurried to the "Dot Store", better know as Target. His heart was set on acquiring a pair of Robot shoes, the latest in the movie craze. We had already spent an hour or more collecting the apparatus for making our own robot. His patience for my other activities on this particular afternoon meant we would make a trip to the Dot Store.

Anna Robertson Brown wrote a thin little book in 1883 entitled, "What is Worthwhile". This little book was translated into many languages and went into 73 printings and stayed in print for 67 years. Why did this little volume become a best seller? Reading an account of this small book made me think of this question of worthiness.

Anna Brown's opening sentences in her small book are riveting: "Only one life to live! We all want to make the most of it. How can we accomplish the most with the energies and power at our command? What is worthwhile?"

Going back to my story, the trip to the Dot store was worthwhile because as I listen to my five-year old nephew, I realized how worthwhile my time was with him. As we passed the lovely profusion of lavender flowers hanging in abundance from the trees, he announced: "Look at the Wisteria! You can't count the blooms because there are too many to count." It's true, you know?

A few short yards later the voice from the back seat revealed another statement worthy of remembering. "JR, (my nickname) I love going anywhere with you." With a lump in my throat, my response was: " I love going anyplace with you too."

I share with the readers the words of Anna Brown. "Seek happiness each day. If you are not happy today, you will never be happy. Strive to be patient, unselfish, purposeful, strong and eager. If you do these things with a grateful heart, you will be happy- at least as happy as it is given man to be on earth."

Be grateful for the happiness that comes in small moments of time. It is all around us in the beauty of nature, the budding and blooming of flowers and trees. It is captured in the words of friends and the expressions of love and enchantment of children. Happiness is a measure of the worthiness of our day and in the efforts we make for our family and our friends.

What is vital or worthwhile to us in this modern day? Are the same guidelines good to go with today? Are we caught up in things and possessions as worthwhile or are we sincere in saying those things that are worthwhile cannot "be seen or held but are felt in the heart"?

Parents have awesome tasks!

The wheel had fallen off the new car the child had gotten for Christmas. With a helpless and forlorn look, the child asked his Dad, "Can you fix it?" Immediately the father took the toy and went to his workshop where he fixed the car good as new.

The teenage girl was dressed for the prom and had snagged her shoe into the hem of her dress. With tears escaping down her cheeks she asked her Mom, "Can you fix it?" With expert hands her mother stitched the hem back in the dress and her daughter went on to the prom.

Over and over again our children ask us, "Can you fix it?" With determination and desire we as parents struggle to fix things for our children and to make their world right once again. We sacrifice for their well-being and make extra efforts to insure their safety. Even though they sometimes rebel against our authority, we still try to fix their lives with health and happiness.

As I think of the moments in time when our children were growing up, there were many occasions when I was disappointed with the fact that I could not fix something for them. They each had to face disappointments; they each had to hurt over a loss of one thing or another. While growing up, each had to experience the anger of having a best friend betray or shun them. In reality, all of these were just incidents of growing up, but at the time, they were devastating to our children.

We as parents think we can indeed fix things for our children. We want to help them make the right choices. We want to give them the benefit of our knowledge. We want to assure them if they follow our instructions, their lives will be much better. As parents, we forget they have a mind of their own and they will make choices we wish they would not.

But this is not just an aspect of parenting, it is also just an aspect of us as individuals. We think we can fix our spouse to be more acceptable to our ideas of the perfect spouse. We believe we can fix our friends and our colleagues so they will be more like we wish them to be. Guess what? We can't!

Fixing people is not possible unless we begin by fixing ourselves. We are the only person we can fix and many times we have trouble even doing that. It is at the time when we realize that fixing the problems around us is often humanly impossible that we become afraid.

And you ask, afraid? Yes afraid! I admit there have been times in my life when I was afraid. I could not fix something for one of our boys or for my husband. With all the desire and determination a person could have, I have had many instances when I was not adequate to fix circumstances in my life. And surely I am not alone in this feeling of inadequacy.

Perhaps accepting the fact that we cannot fix everything is a step in the right direction.

This Mother was a bad teacher!

I watched as a young mother taught her children a lesson. She was in line at a store and I was looking for an item on a nearby shelf. A young man, perhaps only 16, was the cashier, and he was also learning a valuable lesson from the lady. In a moment an assistant manager appeared and she was the recipient of yet another lesson. Very soon the manager of the store came to the checkout counter and learned yet another lesson.

From the moment I walked into the garden section of the store it was apparent that someone had lost control because the voice of a young woman was many decibels above the normal pitch of a calm and mature individual. Her tirade continued for all the customers to witness and grew louder and more aggressive as time lengthened.

I suppose I could have left the area and shopped elsewhere and returned to the garden section later but I was curious as to the outcome of the confrontation. The assistant manager, at first in a kind voice, and later with more persistence, asked the woman to get control of herself because she could not understand her problem. This proved to be a useless instruction.

I have chosen the term woman instead of lady in reference to the episode because I have never witnessed ladies or gentlemen acting in such an immature and irrational manner. The young cashier learned quickly that there are customers who are unreasonable, lack proper upbringing, and are to be tolerated according to store guidelines. It was evident the young man was embarrassed and I could not help but comment to him later about his nice behavior when I checked out.

As I exited the store the young manager was standing with a colleague just outside the door. I stepped up to him and complimented him and his staff on the way they handled the irate woman and responded that her comment to him of a "rude assistant manager" was not accurate.

The episode was ridiculous in many ways. First of all, she was harassing the cashier because he had called for a verification of $10 off on a display microwave and the person from that department did not show. The assistant manager's appearance brought on more words at such volume and speed that she was unable to understand the problem. The episode continued until the manager appeared and got the rest of the outrage with the woman saying she had been standing waiting for the $10 discount for 25 minutes, which was in error also.

I saw once again the rage in a society of parents as the woman's two preschool age children sat in her shopping cart. They witnessed the anger, the uncontrolled behavior of their mother, and the absurdity of the adult who should set example for them to follow. I wondered what kind of anger and punishment they received from her tirades. If this young mother expects her children to have much self control she better learn it herself!

Participating parents

I can still remember my childhood and teen years. I can remember the words, "Sorry, but not today!" A trip to the grocery store was exactly that, a trip to buy groceries. There was a five and dime store where deodorant, cosmetics, and other necessities of life could be purchased. I lived in a real town that had real stores where the hardware, drugstores, movie theater, clothing and furniture stores were all around the square. There was no need to go out of town to buy anything.

A trip to town meant there was no need to beg for anything. Cornflakes or Post Toasties were the only cereals and the newest breakfast treat for children was an amazing innovation called Pop Tarts. Money was scarce and a toy every trip or a meal with drink at a drive through was not even a possibility for good behavior; good behavior was expected without reward.

A small pinch in church, not very painful but enough to get my attention, could make me understand that my wiggling and whispering was to stop immediately or a trip outside would occur. If "looks could kill" a look from my Mother, even from the choir, could stop me in mid-sentence as I sat on the back row with other teenagers. Good behavior, being polite and respectful to adults, was required by my parents.

Extra curricular activities included band, chorus, drama, tennis, track and field events, the annual and newspaper staffs, took place during the six school periods. We had five academic classes and the sixth was a study hall or a selected class of our interest. The "don't pass don't play" was not a rule back then, it didn't have to be. If we didn't pass, we did not do any of the extras in school or after school.

John Rosemond, a North Carolina psychologist wrote in 1996: "Hurting a child's feelings builds conscience". He related a conversation with a mother who did not approve of her husband's discipline. He did not believe in spanking, but according to his wife, "he hurts their feelings". Rosemond replied, "Well, that's the whole idea!"

Discipline does not work unless it hurts the child's feelings. Discipline that causes a little pain or discomfort is valuable. Parents must begin to understand that to some degree they must make a child regret improper behavior. Children are not adults and should not be expected to act as adults. Adults can expect to feel bad if they wrong someone or act inappropriately. Children must be taught by a caring adult to act in an appropriate manner. "The pain creates a permanent memory that serves to inhibit future inappropriate behavior."

Rosemond wrote: "For 30 years American parents at the well-intentioned urging of misguided mental health professionals have been trying to 'make children feel good about themselves'. This notion has created a generation of perpetual children who as adults enter into trial marriages and abandon commitments when reality sets in. They go to work asking not what they can do for the company but what the company can do for them. Breaking the law is no big deal if you can hire a good lawyer."

I believe there are still some parents who believe in punishment for the right reasons and in the right proportions. There are many parents who believe that self-esteem and self-control are possible only if a little pain and discomfort is experienced by children. What works with one child may not work with another, but children must be taught what is expected of them not only by their parents, but by teachers and by society as a whole.

How times have changed!

Since 1960, violent crime has increased at least 560 percent, divorces have more than doubled, and the percentage of children in single-parent homes has tripled. By the year 2000, 40 percent of all American births and 80 percent of minority births will occur out of wedlock.

Elementary students rank near the bottom in tests of math and science. And since 1960, average SAT scores have dropped 75 points in our high schools.

In 1990, teachers listed the top problems in schools as drugs, alcohol, pregnancy, suicide, rape, and assault. Young people no longer feel guilty when they drink and drive, and we can forget about being age 21 before drinking. Smoking is more common than chewing gum and is certainly not a sneak around habit, but one that takes place for anyone to see.

In the decade of the 1990's, Americans murdered 14 million of their own, babies that were killed by their mothers before they took a single breath. The abortion issue didn't seem as important since preventing pregnancies were in pill form. Remember the rule about not killing? Does this include unborn babies or innocent children?

In 2000, about twenty-four percent of Americans said they had lied and cheated on their income tax at an annual cost to the government of about $100 billion. College graduates, one in seven, defaulted on federal college loans. Colleges were turning out people who didn't know the rule about not stealing?

In 2007, a woman, age 101 years was mugged and her $33 stolen. A few blocks away, another elderly lady was beaten and robbed by the same person. Taking care of our elderly does include honoring their longevity and protecting them from harm. Are we outraged? You bet!

The words were: strange, weird, and unbelievable! The media circus continued trying to keep up with the Anna Nicole Smith shenanigans and the burial of James Brown. As the burial ceremonies for these two people began to take place, last but not least were the words "family greed".

Justice Roy Moore stood firm about the display of the Ten Commandments in 2003 and gave up his judgeship as proof of his belief. Moments later the media pounced upon him and derided his stand as being less than smart. He faded into history as a man who said the "Ten" should make a difference in our country.

A minister once remarked that he would preach against sin if he could determine what qualified. We are living in the media age when instant accounts of "what is happening" in the world are at our fingertips. With all of the statistics and media attention to the details of society available to everyone, is it any wonder that we can ignore the seriousness of the faults and failures of our celebrities?

Train parents to train children

A child was screaming at the top of his lungs. Oh wow, was he ever screaming! It was late morning when many people try to do their main shopping because their energy level has not diminished. Therefore, as the buggies rolled silently and the shoppers scanned the shelves for their needs, the wailing child seemed even louder.

Being around children and watching them pitch tantrums over the years, I shrugged my shoulders and hurriedly chose items from my list and rushed to check out. I found long ago it is easier to avoid a situation than it is to tolerate some of them. Knowing the child was just beginning to hit his prime scream level, exiting the store was certainly the answer for me.

As I placed items from my cart on the conveyor belt, the cashier rolled her eyes upward knowing she did not have the same solution that I had, escape! Just then the young dad moved toward the counter struggling to control the three year old child in his arms. Kicking and screaming, the child did not seem to be running low on energy. The young dad looked horrified and embarrassed at the scene his child was making.

Needless to say, my sympathy was not only for him but also for the child. Our attitude of proper discipline for temper tantrums has changed making it impossible for parents to handle unruly behavior in public. If they ignore the situation, it does not go away! If they discipline their child, they run the risk of being charged with child cruelty.

As I exited the store the father and child were right behind me. The child had not relented in his screaming for at least five to ten minutes. With a look from the father of:

"what would you do", I got in my car, but I didn't stop feeling sorry for both father and child.

Why the child you may ask? I know that in the near future teachers and other adults will have to deal with this child who cannot control his own behavior. His parents will soon get letters from school that tell them their child has been labeled. He will find then himself in a special behavior modification program. If not, the child will eventually have an unsavory reputation among school staff.

The same week in another location, I rushed over to a child in the aisle of a large department store. My fear was that she was lost because her screams of alarm were frightening. Another lady reached her at the same time and like myself, she thought the child was lost from her mother.

By the time we both reached the three year old child, a young lady with a stroller reached her also, her mother. The mother seemed surprise at our attention. She had been ignoring the temper fit and was allowing the child to scream and holler at the top of her lungs.

The other shopper and myself walked slowly away shaking our heads in confusion. I took my purchases to the salesman who was too distracted by the incident to immediately take my merchandise even though I am sure he worked on a commission. He said, "Parents don't raise children the same anymore."

While I understand the young mother's technique of trying to modify the child's behavior, I also realized it was not working. The young mother had said "no" to her child and had proceeded to ignore an even worse behavior, that of pitching a fit in the store.

If you observe the behavior of children in public places like I often do, it will surprise you at the new techniques of behavior training that are not working. When a child screams in anger for many minutes because she refuses to accept the answer from her parent, the technique is certainly not working.

Needless to say, all parents go through the trials and errors of learning discipline techniques as they try to discover the right way to teach their child. What works for one child will not work for all children. What helps a child learn self-control and self-discipline will not work for everyone. It is the pursuit of the right way to teach children self-value and self-discipline that is important in the long run.

The young mother, while showing she was in charge of her child, chose a busy department store of strangers to teach her child the consequences of her wrong behavior. She was ignored! While the screams went on and on other shoppers were quick to surmise the child was lost.

Did the technique work? No! The young mother gave into the child and took her to get the item the child had wanted just to quiet her down. After all the misbehavior, her mother rewarded the child for pitching a fit. The idea was a good one for the child in the beginning, but the results of her mother giving in to her demands erased the lesson quickly.

I read this: "Children today love luxury too much. They have detestable manners, flout authority, have no respect for their elders. They no longer rise when their parents or teachers enter the room. What kind of awful creatures will they be when they grow up?" The scholar who wrote these words was Socrates, shortly before his death in 339B.C. Things have not changed very much have they?

When are you a parent?

Everyone knows you arrive early at the Fourth of July Parade if you want a front row seat. So, they did! People carried their folding chairs several blocks and got a perfect place to see it all. Others arrived later and arranged their seats to the side and behind the earlier crowd. Perfect seats until the parade approached, then young people, with their parents watching, stood up in front of those seated people blocking the view entirely.

No one bothered to tell the youngsters to sit down or move out from in front of the adults. Parents ignored the rude behavior of their children and those who had arrived early hesitated to ask them to move not knowing the response they might get from rude parents as well as the rude children.

Likewise, everyone loves the fair and every year the crowds are exceptional. The events, rides, and the exhibits were fascinating to us old "stick in the muds". Young children were fascinated with a life-size robot that appeared to move on his own and could carry on a conversation with them.

Young children would gently pat the robot on his mid section and then fall back as the robot would giggle or move his arms. One young girl, not so young that she couldn't understand that her behavior was inappropriate, kept jabbing at the neck and face of the robot. Younger children were horrified at her continued behavior.

A man standing a short distance away controlled the mind and the mouth of the robot. He was unobtrusive and kept the children believing the robot could speak to them. The harassing from the girl escalated despite the continuing remarks from the robot to leave him alone and not hit him again.

Finally in desperation, the "robot man" speaking through the robot asked a woman if she was the girl's mother. When she responded that she was, much to the delight of the crowd, the robot said: "Why don't you act like it?"

People will often tolerate some inappropriate behavior from children if their parents are not watching them closely. Politely, adults will caution children about being kind and respecting the rights of others. At times, a familiar youngster will be corrected if it is known their parents expect them to behave.

But what do you do when parents are watching them? What mortifies older adults is that parents will stand by and watch their children not only show disrespect for adults but also for their own friends. "Are you a parent?"

Nothing New Under the Sun!

The saying that "there is nothing new under the sun" needs a slight amount of revising. The Internet for example has enabled us to fascinate, and entertain children for hours. The main problem is that we may not know exactly how they are being entertained and fascinated because we are not Internet savvy.

Take for example, the Ipod and the MP3 player. I purchased one for our niece but couldn't help her with putting music on it. A much younger person will need to to help her program this latest advance in technology.

Electric locks on my car doors were a real advancement for me. When I realized the trunk could be opened from the inside with a button or with the little black rectangle attached to my key ring, I was really fascinated.

A friend showed me that she could push a button and the door on her van would open. Then she revealed that the back seats in the van would disappear into the floor with the push of another button. Of course, knowing the temperature on the outside is another feature on new cars while I'm just concerned with whether the heater inside my car is working.

While walking through a parking lot I heard a ringing sound as a car nearly cut me down as I walked behind it. Then, I became aware that the ringing was a warning mechanism on new cars that let unsuspecting pedestrians know they were about to be run over by an automobile.

We are living in an enlightened age when everything is done by machine. We have treadmills that help us walk to nowhere, stair climbers that do not take us up, rowing machines without having any water, and bicycles that can't take us around the block or up the street.

A few years ago Ninja turtles, Power Rangers and Barbie dolls were the fads. Now Transformers, Furbies that interact with the child in your house, and robots and raptors parade around the house. We were fascinated with the wetsy Betsy a few years ago until a doll was on the market that could give birth to a baby with the twist of a knob.

It has become quite fascinating to the older generation as we see the changes in today's world of high tech. A grandmother thought her four-year-old grandchild was brilliant when he could count from 20 to zero backwards. When she asked if he learned that in school, he told her he learned it from the microwave.

The man of our house still has trouble with the VCR so don't ask him about a DVD. All he knows is that his television is messed up and he can't fix it if that machine under it has a red light on. Don't ask him about computers. He thinks of them as electric typewriters with a solitaire game. Don't ask him about fax machines. He does accept them but had much rather have signatures in blue ink in his hand.

There should be classes for those of us who can't figure out how to move into this century with high tech machines.

Who is confused?

My brother said never to start a plumbing project unless the hardware store was open. Having just finished a water feature in my yard, I realized the wisdom of his words. I had ten different receipts for plumbing supplies I had purchased only to find I needed something else. Thus when the project was completed there were numerous parts to return.

The men who worked in the plumbing departments were always willing to help the poor lady who was looking confused in numerous aisles. I would attempt to tell them about my project and being helpful gentlemen, they patiently listened, looking confused, and would give what help they thought I needed.

Most of the parts I returned were ones they had helped me determine I needed. Try telling someone you are plumbing a clay pot for your garden and you need to go from the inch and a quarter hole in the bottom to a three quarter piece at the top of the pot. Add to this requirement that you needed them to screw together rather than be glued and watch the expressions change to confusion again.

"Why didn't you just buy the pot ready made for a water feature," the man of the house said. "It wouldn't be so much 'fun' if it was ready made," I said. "I think you just like to confuse those sales people at the hardware stores," he remarked. "So far, they are still confused so I must be doing a good job of confusing," I reply.

I come from a long line of "piddlers". If you aren't familiar with the term it means I can spend days figuring out how to do something, realize that isn't what I want to do and spend several more days determining what to do next. My Dad taught me how to piddle away a day or so on a project and make everyone watching think I was accomplishing something important. He was a "master piddler" and I learned from him.

There is an art to being a piddler. You can spend hours piddling instead of being bored wondering what you are going to do to occupy your day. It is especially useful for retired men who do not know what to do with all that extra time they have when they aren't cutting the grass. You get a lot of exercise because you never have the right tools handy and you make many trips back and forth to the toolbox.

You do however, get a great deal of satisfaction out of finally finishing a project no one thought you would ever finish. You put a smile on the faces of cashiers when you innocently remark, "I'm not sure which of these receipts are for these parts, but they are on one in this stack!"

Cell Phone Mania

"I tried to call you on your cell phone." I respond," I didn't have it on!" Again a statement from the man of our house, "I tried to call you on your cell phone. Why didn't you turn it on?" I reply, "It was turned on, I left it in the car." He asked another question, "Why do you have a cell phone if you never answer it?" Being honest with him, I answer, "So you can call me."

This is a question and answer session we have on a regular basis. I don't always remember to turn the phone on and most often, it is in the car and I'm not! I could have told the "man of the house" that I really had it so I could call him and not necessarily for him to have the same opportunity.

The invention of the portable phones and the cell phone/camera/video/ Black something or other, makes for instant communication. These inventions also mean you have no time to be quiet, be thoughtful, be unhurried, or non-communicative. You are strapped to those infernal status symbols and apparently no one wants to be out of touch with anyone in the world.

Being out of reach is often very good. I see young mothers trying to communicate in grocery stores, hung over meat counters, stretching up to high shelves, and with her fifth sense and third hand, she is trying to corral two active children. If you eavesdrop on her conversation it more than likely is a multitasking job of catching up on the latest gossip or family disagreement.

I find it quite difficult to keep up with the latest advancements from the telecommunication industry. I still feel guilty if I am talking on the phone and it beeps for another incoming call. Rather than answer the new call I usually ignore it. I hate making two people feel I don't want to talk with them. Friends and family know to call back unless they get the answer machine.

Most people check caller id and decide whether to answer or not. I look to see with whom I get to talk and whether to be excited or harassed because it is one more "privacy number" soliciting some information or donation. When I recognize the number I get a quick surge of anticipation because a friend or family member is checking on us or calling with news.

Then came the caller id and it proved to be a great addition to our home phone. Now I know how many times the man of the house tries to get me during the day and who else is looking for me. The only disadvantage is the stored up numbers that also tell how many times I have been on the phone that took all my time away from running "his" errands.

I will probably be a while before I conform to the take your cell phone, turn it on, and don't leave it in the car commands. At least I have the cell phone status symbol if I want to use it.

Technology Passes By

It has become a habit over the years to have one or more electronic gadgets running in our household at all times. It may be a radio, a computer, a cassette tape or the latest, a compact disk. Even trips to the stores include a "look through" of the latest in movies on DVD.

I listened to the term "parental guide" being explained by the technology on cable and other television hook ups. It seems that the networks have stopped policing their shows and handed down that responsibility to parents. Of course, this is a refreshing idea, parents being in charge of what they allow their children to view. Somebody needs to tell them!

The popular song of some years ago, "Ain't Nobody's Business but My own" has been successfully erased by the likes of Jerry Springer, Maury, Oprah, and Montel. Every odd couple, eccentric individual, or pervert in the United States has a chance of appearing on these programs. Those not on talk shows can be on court shows.

If you are guilty of having an affair with a relative, a teenage boy who beats his girlfriend for fun, do not know the parent of your child, find yourself in an abusive relationship and loving it, you too could have a spot on one of these shows.

We all thought the "runaway bride" in 2006 was a big item until later he middle-aged woman who had the child by her teenage husband in Gainesville, Georgia, was really big news and TV show material. Then, we could put our former State School Superintendent on the air to tell about her facelift with stolen money and her experiences while serving the next 8 years in jail. Now, those are big deals.

Just think, if the airwaves could get dirty and stay that way indefinitely from the language and absurdity of talk shows, would we not suffocate? If these weird, unnatural, immoral, ridiculous, and unusual relationships are the norm of American society, are we not in trouble?

Family secrets that were safely guarded in former generations, has become the latest attraction for television audiences. It is appalling to know that we take delight in watching this kind of behavior exploited and called entertainment. It is refreshing to watch Regis Philbin and have Kelly Rippa talk about her rescuing a baby bird at her son's summer camp.

Hot wedding

Hot weather makes my mind wanders back to August 1961. It was so hot that year the water from the garden hose came out as steam. There was a bowl of water for the dog that we kept filled at all times, but it was so hot the dog wouldn't drink it. The genteel ladies quit perspiring and started sweating like all the rest of us.

Can you imagine the dread of having to dress up for church services knowing you were going to an un-air conditioned church? Just think of a wedding at 4 pm! Of course, the windows would come up, but for a wedding with lighted candles, the windows down front would be closed.

Think about the guys in tuxedos and the girls in the wedding party with their hair in various styles plastered down with hair spray. Can you imagine how they would look and feel by 4 pm? Can you imagine the looks of "I can't believe you would choose the hottest month of the year to get married"?

It was a mere 90 degrees in the shade where the relatives waited to go into the church. All the aunts had their dainty little fans and their handkerchiefs would wave in rhythm with the fan. The uncles stood around in a bunch acting like they were use to the heat while the water dripped from the tip of their noses.

Inside the church in a small room used as a nursery on Sundays, the girls in the wedding party fanned the bride. Electric fans circulated the hot air all around her feet, careful not to aim air toward her face for fear it would mess up her hairdo. Makeup was not the norm for the bride so no swipe was made to get the perspiration from her face. The water was allowed to drip until the last minute.

Four o'clock arrived and the crowd in the church was ready to get things over and done with. It seems the organist put the wedding march in double time so the service would be over shortly. The preacher started cutting out phrases in his mind leaving just enough words to make sure he had all the bases covered in the vows.

By eleven minutes after the hour the wedding party was exiting the church headed for the punch bowl only to be called back for the hastily made pictures. Everyone was trying their best to smile for pictures. The photographer's assistant was kept busy wiping down the wedding party, especially the obvious sweat from the bride's face. It had changed from perspiration to downright sweat by then.

Looking back to that summer wedding makes me think that the church members decided right then and there that air conditioning the church was a must. It was no longer necessary for the minister to preach on the prospects of hell being hot for sinners. All he had to mention was an August wedding at 4 pm.

Pieces that do not fit

Have you ever noticed that when you think you have a comfortable life there are pieces that do not quite fit? And have you ever stop to realize that what is comfortable to one person may not be comfortable to another?

If you paint the woodwork, the walls will need a coat of paint. When the walls are clean and freshly painted the ceiling looks dark and dingy. Once the room is painted, the chair looks shabby and the sofa needs recovering and lamps do not fit like they should. One simple change, one small task has placed the surroundings in disarray.

Move a skirted table and the items stored underneath must be relocated. Buy a new piece of furniture and the room must be rearranged to accommodate it. Try a new look in a room and all the other decorations seem to lose their importance in the scheme of things. Paint and change has caused areas not to fit together as they once did.

Husbands will never understand a woman's need to redecorate and change the house. They fail to realize the recliner is crooked from the broken metal levers because it still feels okay. They do not see the smudge marks left by hands that have soiled the arms as they pushed back for their evening nap, and woe be the woman who suggests a new chair rather than reupholstering the old one.

Most men are just alike. They have a nice sports coat so why buy a new one. "Those shoes don't look bad they just need to be polished, and they are the most comfortable ones I have! There is no need for me to get new underwear until this wears out. Yes, the elastic is stretched, they are thread bare in places, and under the arms are beyond bleaching, but I like them and, they are comfortable." Sound familiar?

Why is it that women love change and men fight it? Why are we always wanting a new something or other and men are satisfied with what they have? Why are we forever bemoaning the fact that our house needs updating and men are always wondering why and what is the cost of updating? Is the comfort level of men and women different? You bet it is!

This same reference moves into other areas. Women have nothing to wear and need to buy a complete new wardrobe; men are satisfied with the old suit if it fits, and a new tie. Women may or may not like their latest hair cut, color or perm; men are satisfied as long as their hair is staying on their heads and not coming off in the shower. Women wear shoes for looks and men wear shoes for comfort. Women switch grocery stores and shopping places to see what is new; men are most comfortable in familiar surroundings and see no need to change if the price is right.

Life indeed has its comfort zones for us. Lest we be deceived into believing we are comfortable with the "places" in our lives we should remember that no sooner do we think we have assembled a comfortable life than we find a piece of ourselves that has no place to fit in. It happens to us all.

Grandmothers are grand!

In doing research for a study project, I was amazed to read that at one time, seven, and eight generations of people knew each other. Of course, they lived to be from 600 to 950 years of age. Think of all the birthday presents grandparents had to buy. Just think of all the stuff their children had to discard after 900 years of collecting.

It is a rarity these days when we are privileged to know four generations of the same family. With the transient lifestyles of most families, and children moving further and further from their birthplaces, it is surprising that we are even acquainted with a whole generation of people.

The heritage generally passed down from earlier generations is now lost to many families. Grandparents live in different states, across a country, or in another country, and their visits with grandchildren are few and far between. Some families can only share pictures with each other because traveling on a regular basis is prohibitive. Families must find close friends and acquaintances who are good influences and can show their children the character traits of an older generation.

My grandparents lived just down the street. We spent as much time in their house as we did at our own. Grandmother would always have those delicious warm teacakes and ice-cold milk for snacks and we became well versed in when the teacakes would be ready for eating. Even if we were hard at play, the smell would drift upward and over to our yard. Immediately the request to go to Grandmother's would be made.

My own memories are of my own Grandmother who was very tall and stately. She was slender and she wore her hair in a bun at the back of her head. At night she would release the hair and it hung to her waist. She would sit and comb and comb her long hair while I sat on the bed and watched.

My visits to her house were always a treat, not because she had gifts or surprises but because she was there with my Granddaddy. Their house was filled with surprises that would interest any curious four year old. With the rule being "look, but do not touch" instilled into all of us children, a walk through the house was a place of enchantment.

For sure, I recall the attitudes and character traits of my grandparents. While they were conservative they were also generous. They were strong in mind and spirit, but gentle and kind in nature. They were faithful and trustworthy in their friendships and their self- discipline made them hard workers. They were worthy of praise and wonderful influences to us growing up.

In Toni Morrison's book, "The Bluest Eyes", Claudia tells of her lack of enthusiasm for the dolls she always got for Christmas. She bemoans the fact that the adults are so happy she has gotten the doll they had wanted when they were young. It does not impress Claudia that they would have been very happy.

Claudia is a ten-year-old living in a poor rural setting. She is not delighted with the trappings of gifts. Her idea of the perfect gift would be to sit in her grandmother's kitchen on a stool, eat her fresh baked cookies and have her granddaddy play his guitar and sing, just for her.

Grandmothers today have more things, more toys, and more surprises than we had as children. The collector dolls, the latest and greatest collectables for boys line the shelves and fill the toy boxes, but the toys are quickly forgotten by the children as the next series becomes available. Would sitting in the kitchen and eating fresh baked cookies and listening to music be exciting for them?

Birthday time each year for our sons meant their grandmother would ask what they would like from her? The answer was always the same, a caramel cake just for them. Of course, they did not expect to eat it all by themselves but the cake was there each year for those special occasions. Even now, when birthdays come around, their wish is that "Grandmother was still here and could fix them a caramel cake."

Have we grown too used to the dolls and the trappings of a fast paced world to appreciate the simple pleasures we enjoyed as children? Do grandmothers remember?

Phrases can remain a lifetime

There are a great many rules that are taught to youngsters that they will never use. Likewise, there are quite a few rules and reasons youngsters will hear that stick with them for a lifetime. Youngsters look forward to the magical time in their lives when they can do as they please, but alas, there is no such time.

Mother's favorite rule was: "Never leave home without clean underwear. You may be in an accident." My thoughts immediately turned to the fact that surely if I was injured in an accident my underwear would not need medical attention and a doctor would not say, "Don't help this girl her underwear is not clean!"

"Don't get your clothes dirty until after church", another rule. My clothes rarely found places at church to get dirty. Anyhow, everyone knew having fun at church was against the rules, therefore no dirty clothes. Besides, we knew dirty clothes at church was a sin.

"Quit squirming!" When your pants are too tight or your skirt is 100% wool and you forgot your slip, you squirm. If you are six years old you squirm a lot and you can't help this action under the best of conditions.

"Don't play with your food!" Any smart child knows that food does not play. Jello is difficult to manage, but spinach does play, you just have difficulty making your fork cooperate with your mouth. After a short lesson from older siblings you know to push your food around on your plate so your parents think you have eaten a sufficient amount of healthy stuff.

"I told you it would break!" This is the next phrase after the words, "I knew you would get hurt>" How do parents know things will happen before they happen? Their words didn't help the hurt feelings or the intense pain. The don't do's always came after the already did's in my case.

I can still hear echoes from, "This is the last time I am going to tell you," but it never was the last time because I kept forgetting the first 1000 times.

When nothing else could answer a question, the usual response was: "Because I said so!" This answer put an end to polite conversation real quick. It did not answer the aforementioned question, but it sure made things final.

"You'll understand when you have children of your own." I didn't want to wait until I had children to get my answer because I needed some reasonable excuse then. Children learned very soon to be very slow to answer the question "Who did that?" I always hated the next sentence, especially if I was the guilty party, "If someone doesn't admit it, all of you will be punished." That was always a sure sign someone would be a tattle tale.

Waiting for the cake to Cool

My Mother loved to cook but seldom had enough time to pursue her pleasures in the kitchen. The flower shop that was in our back yard was a constant distraction with customers coming even after the shop was closed. A knock on the backdoor and Mother would have to stop a meal, turn off the stove and go to the shop to "fix just a little something for me to take to the hospital".

She never needed to ask our children what they wanted for their birthday because their answer was always the same. Her cake with caramel icing was always their request. If she knew we were making a trip to Cartersville for a visit, she hurriedly fixed a cake or some treat for the children before we arrived.

I was always amazed at how she could "throw a meal together" on such short notice. We would be driving in the driveway an hour or so after our call and she would be putting a whole meal on the table with fresh baked bread and all.

I am often reminded of the ways we use to function. There was not a hurried trip to the deli or to the big "ready to serve" counters in the grocery stores. There were quart jars of green beans prepared from the garden each year and soup mixture because daddy always had more tomatoes than he could give away. When we finally got a freezer, the other delights from the garden were eaten all winter.

We have become a last minute society. We plan a hurried trip to the store to pick up a meal or we eat at restaurants or fast food establishments. Having homemade biscuits or cornbread is a real treat and to have a cake made from "scratch" instead of in a plastic container is a total surprise to children.

Around our house the meal on Sunday is usually one when we return to the old fashion way of cooking. Fresh green beans, fried okra, corn on the cob, and fried chicken are the usual fare, or some such menu. A cake, pie, or even a fresh fruit cobbler is sometimes the dessert unless everyone is dieting again.

We are a hurried people. We run the caution lights, blow our horns to prompt people to move faster, or blink our lights for them to get out of our way. In a checkout line we shift from foot to foot and look at the people who are slowing us up, especially those who have to have a price check.

Do we ever have time for the cake to cool? This is a question I have asked before and will surely ask again. Are we missing the opportunities to sit around the kitchen table with our family and slice pieces of warm cake and drink a glass of milk or a cup of coffee? Are those pleasures of "homemade" fading into the memories of the past? Not in every household!

Daddy was a piddler

My dad was a piddler and a tinkerer. He could fix any piece of machinery. Our lawn mower was so old that the manufacturer didn't even recognize the model. It still ran and still cut the grass.

Every year daddy had a big garden in the smallest space imaginable. His tiller was so old we thought Noah, from the ark, had probably been its first owner. Daddy had gotten it from a friend who purchased a newer model. Of course, after Daddy got it purring like a kitten, the original owner wanted to buy it back.

Daddy strung his pole beans on actual poles of bamboo he cut down at the creek. He would disappear one morning and return with his truck full of fresh cut cane. For several days he would gently attach the growing wines of beans onto the canes and when they were fully laden with beans he could walk under the canopy of wines and pick the beans.

We had green beans! Did we ever have green beans? There was a harvest each day from his vines strung on the bamboo canes. Walking beneath the vines he could pick enough for a meal or to can or freeze. We never seemed to run out of green beans all through the winter months. Of course, it never seemed convenient for the big yield of beans, but Mother would stop in her busy day to "put them up" so they would not be wasted.

I was the proud owner of a 20-year-old Ford car. It got me to college and back many times but there were many weekends when Daddy and I would work on it to make sure I could make the 30 mile trip back to school on

Sunday. I was always right under him as he tinkered with one thing or another on that car.

My father spent hours on our old car. He tinkered with the oil filters, the radiator, checked the tires and made sure the brake fluid was up to the line. I can see him now, or at least his feet and legs sticking out from under the car. He made sure it was safe to drive and would last until the loan was paid. As we got older and started driving he made sure we too knew how to check out the car.

Daddy had all kinds of stories to tell if we would ever stop long enough to listen. His grandfather was a blacksmith and he often told of inventions he made to help his wife do her work because she could not walk well. His own dad was an entrepreneur of sorts because he could trade anything to anybody for a better deal.

I remember Daddy telling about Grandfather buying the same Jeep over and over again after the war and always making money in the trade. Another favorite story was that he sold a bunch of hogs he bought while sitting in front of the dry good store. He made a profit on the hogs and never got up off the bench and never saw the hogs.

?

What about those tomatoes

There are parts of our personality, character, and abilities that are inherited. Daddy was pretty sharp when it came to machinery and making things just as his Granddaddy. He could plow and farm as well as his own Dad and many times he excelled in his endeavors by raising produce much bigger than usual, like a five-pound green bean.

My brothers often remarked how thy believed they had inherited part of the Roper abilities to fix things and create new items. I don't believe the inheriting is past down strictly from one male generation to another. I can fix things and often even have pieces left over. Most of the time the machinery still operates.

Marjorie Holmes wrote a delightful book entitled "I've Got to Talk to Somebody, God". She expresses appreciation for the simple things of her life and in so doing, she revealed a deep understanding of what was important to her growing up.

She writes: "Please help me learn the simple secrets of making a bed. However I try, there are always these bumps and wrinkles, or something trailing, and the pillows never quite match." She continues to write that she is thankful that her children have nice comfortable beds and clean sheets. They did not have to sleep on mud floor, or huddled like animals on city streets.

She writes that she does not have to peel potatoes as often as her mother or her grandmother but she reminds the reader how fortunate she felt to have food on the table even though some vegetables were not her favorites.

I remember my brother saying over and over again that he did not like tomatoes. Well, tomatoes were a way of life around our house in the summertime. My Dad was the champion tomato grower in Bartow County harvesting enough to feed his family and deliver to people all over town who would brag on his yield.

Holmes wrote of potatoes, dusty, dirty, earth colored potatoes. They were "humble, plain, yet holding within their white flesh the stuff of life for our survival. The miracle of nourishment."

Baked, fried, boiled, or eaten raw with salt was okay by her, but today we zip by the fast food places and grab French fries for hungry kids. French fries and burgers are the soul food for children and teens and this vegetable is still the miracle of nourishment for most of them.

With fast foods we have turned into a wasteful society. Wrappers from fast food places, bottles and drink cans fill our yard each week, and as traffic increases so does the liter. We spend a lot of time picking up the wastefulness of the people who pass our house and we are often surprised at the items we find.

The incidents in our lives, called experience by the experts, determine many times how we will react, or how we will choose. People who grew up in the depression years and the years following World War II are prone to make things last and to take care of those hard earned luxuries.

I love to place a vision in my mind of my Dad standing in his small garden surveying its bounty. His innovations for caring and tending his garden never ceased to amaze the other gardeners in the community.

But my appreciation was those tomatoes fresh from the garden. Just the thought of a good tomato sandwich spread lavishly with mayo makes my mouth water and my senses come alive. I can still see those tomato cages ringed in pine straw to keep the tomatoes from touching the ground. I can almost taste the warmth of a fresh picked tomato ripened by the summer sun.

My Labor was too Cheap!

Mother and Daddy had a greenhouse in Cartersville for 27 years. I just simply hated the fact that every holiday and every time I wanted to do something special we had to work in the flower shop.

I wish now that I had listened once in a while to either one of them as they explained the right and wrong ways to plant shrubs, flowers or vegetables. But, what teenager listens when their minds are befuddled with non-essential information?

Daddy would already have planted the seeds in flats for the spring garden rush. He would point to a shovel and a frame with hardware cloth stretched over it, and give the instructions: "Go sift some dirt!"

When we first move to the house where the greenhouse was located there was a five-foot bank all around the back of the shop. I don't exaggerate when I say that 27 years later there was not a sign of a bank but the area where we used to dig was a few inches below ground level. We would dig in the bank throw the dirt at the wire frame and "sift the dirt".

The next chore was to take that flat of tomato plants; Daddy grew the best plants around, and plant them in cups. Daddy would say: "see those three flats of tomato plants?" We didn't want to say we saw them but it was too obvious to deny. "Well, they need to be ready for the rush in two weeks so get busy."

I never quite understood how God could put plants together that tight in all of those flats. There must have been a hundred plants to the inch and more paper cups than we could count ready for filling and planting.

The price of the cups would be about 10 cents and that was another confusion to me as a teenager. I had helped sift the dirt, planted all those little sprouts into paper cups and we had millions lined up for the gardeners. My time was worth lots more than 10 cents a cup, or at least I thought so!

Every spring when the fields are being plowed and the farmers and gardeners are looking at the newest and best plants and seeds for their gardens, I remember filling wheelbarrows full of "sifted" dirt, planting tomatoes by the millions and all for one thin dime.

The price for experience was sure cheap in my youth. Now the newest and latest techniques for growing tomato plants is a $75 magic box that sits on the patio and produces more tomatoes than the neighborhood can consume. But don't ask me about the magic. I get hung up on sifting dirt.

Growing up in the 50's

I often write that growing up in the 50's and 60's was tough, but it really wasn't until I count the number of years that have passed since then. I have noticed that I now act, feel, and talk like an old timer. I often stumble across the reality that I am out of touch with the issues and answers of socially acceptable behavior.

Teenagers were making marriage plans after graduating from high school in the 50's. They were mature and ready to begin living happily ever after and the reality is that they are still living happily with their original spouse. If we check the newspapers each week for announcements, there are many about fifty-year anniversaries.

We all thought we were grown up when we graduated from high school at the ripe old age of eighteen. Later we knew that we were not grown until many years later. Boys were going into the military as draftees and girls were waving goodbye to the love of their lives. Many of those young men never returned and others returned with severe medical problems.

There was a code of ethics that kept us from associating with individuals with bad reputations. We protected our friends of course and would never lie, but avoiding the truth was our way of not betraying their trust. Needless to say, we didn't have drugs and alcohol at our fingertips, but some of the boys could get a beer or two to pass around on occasion.

Sex was discussed only in the company of our closest friends, and the discussions were brief and uninformed. What we knew was filtered through library books in the dark corners of the public library. The librarian stood guard to make sure none of us underage kids had access to some books.

Some boys you did not date because they would tell tales that were not true. Some girls, boys would date only after dark and then they were careful not to be seen by their friends. If a girl found herself "in a family way", she went to live with a relative in another town far, far away.

A big date in the fifties was to go to the drive-in movie with two or more couples piled into the car. After the movie we all gathered at Beck's Drive-in for cokes and the best hotdogs in town. The whole evening for the boy would cost about $5 and would take him all weekend to earn enough for another date the next week.

I know that at times references to my generation are prudish, naïve, old fashion, and we are always told to "get real". I think we are all of those things with common sense, good judgment, family pride, and our commitments are real and important. Growing up in the 50's and 60's wasn't so tough after all!

Big Family in Small House

A trip to Cartersville, Georgia meant I would drive by the house that was home to me for many years. The huge cedar tree we always planned to decorate at Christmas is no longer there. It was a six foot tree when we moved to the house, but as years passed it became large enough and shaped just right to have been the "Great Tree" on top of the downtown Rich's store.

For a family of six, the house looks extremely small to me now. We shared rooms with each other because separate bedroom for each child was impossible. There was a set of bunk beds my Dad built and the one sleeping on top could almost touch his nose to the ceiling without taking his head off his pillow.

The kitchen was also the dining room and the gathering place for family discussions, homework, and table games. The den was so small if you sat on the sofa to watch television you could prop your feet on the wall across from it. The television did not take up much room because it was so small we stained to see it from the doorway of the kitchen because seating was a premium.

Heating the house was done with gas heaters in each room and they never seemed adequate. To save on gas during the winter Mother would hang a sheet over the doorframes and close off the bedrooms. Needless to say, getting children out of warm beds to dress for school on chilly mornings was a real chore to Mother.

The first one to the heater in the kitchen got the choice spot to warm his or her backside. If you stood too close, or too long, your legs became dark and ugly red and this would last well past school time. Classmates would remark about how our legs looked like lobster legs. At that time in my life I probably didn't think that was so bad since lobster was an unknown creature of the deep blue seas.

You probably aren't interested too much in what was inside our house, but you can probably identify with the meager surroundings of the fifties and sixties. There were rugs on creaky floors, some rooms had doors, and others did not. No window would lock and the breeze that came in around them in winter was like having an air conditioner. In the summer, a window unit or fan would struggle to cool one room ten degrees.

Generally there was a smell of a cake baking or some other tantalizing odor stirring our hunger to fever pitch. Mother would be standing by the stove in her apron mixing and fixing for the ravenous children who would be home each night for dinner.

Growing up, I didn't notice these features of the house. The house didn't seem so small, at least not all the time. Those walls could still tell tales of our family and the memories they made together. At the time we were poor, but we didn't really know that fact. Remembering the house and the family makes me feel rich now.

Grandfather was a trader!

My Grandfather was a farmer by trade. He grew up around Fairmount and Jasper, Georgia. He was a colorful character even to me, a child. He was gruff at times and I don't recall ever seeing much of a smile on his face, a bit frightening to a small child. His face reflected a hard life and was creased and weather worn from long years of farming. I know from conversations with my Dad that his father was often a hard man to understand.

Grandfather was well known as a trader. For several years after the war, he bought and sold the same jeep many times, always making money on both the purchase and selling prices. The tale is told that he was sitting with a group of farmers in front of the Mercantile store in Jasper when another farmer approached him about buying some pigs. Grandfather made him a price. The pigs, sight unseen, but before he left town a few hours later, he had sold the pigs to another farmer, at a profit.

Any reference to his ability to make a "good trade" always resulted in statements concerning the special skills needed for trading, but the most important aspect, he said, was knowing what to keep and what to trade.

While I was still in high school my Grandfather passed away. He was still a colorful character at age 87. He had plowed his 2-acre garden that year with a team of mules and only claimed to be a little sore from the rope around his shoulders.

Our lives are constantly filled with "trading" situations. We may be asked to trade our principles for a little more profit. We may be faced with a proposal that would trade our integrity and reputation for position and fame. In the social world we are often called upon to trade loyalty for prestige, character for credibility, idle chitchat for gossip. In the world of power, business and politics, people are called upon to trade friends for the right acquaintances, facts for fabrications, and right for wrong as they are forced to hide behind a facade of deception to win the accolades of people they do not even respect.

How difficult we seem to want to make the situations of life where the choices should be simple, where loyalty and right from wrong should take precedence over prestige, power and position. Over and over in the course of our lifetime we will ask ourselves these questions: What am I willing to trade? What is worth keeping and what am I willing to exchange?

I have among my collections these words about The Philosopher: "I saw him sitting in his door, trembling as old men do; his house was old, his barn was old, and yet his eyes seemed new. His eyes had seen three times my years, and kept a twinkle still, though they had looked at birth and death and three graves on a hill. 'I will sit down with you and you will make me wise; tell me how you have kept the joy still burning in your eyes?' Then like an old time orator, impressively he rose. 'I make the most of all that comes, and the least of all that goes!' "

Time slips away

Words of wisdom often come to me through conversations and are so good that I must pass them along. Of course, most of my words of wisdom are preceded by the phrase, "Mother use to say…." And the words just spill out from my mouth and my mind.

This time, however, my listener passed along the best gem of wisdom when she remarked, "When you hear your words coming out of the mouths of your own children you know you have taught them some of your principles.

I am very much aware of how our thoughts and our actions move from generation to generation. Young parents struggle with the latest behavior patterns that seem to emerge with each generation. They then discover, after a time, that their own parents experienced the same unexpected behavior in them.

No, we did not have as many tragic accidents when we were growing up but there was a very good reason. We did not have access to a vehicle except on special occasions and it was the family car. No, we did not drive fast and we paid more attention to how close we were to other cars because the absence of the family car touched each one of us.

We did not have to convince our parents that we should date at 13. The rules of all parents were the same. We could go with a boy to chaperoned school functions when we were 15 and car dates at 16. "Don't even ask," was our philosophy, because it would do no good. Parents had a great network of passing rules between them

Sometimes I find myself remarking that I am "sort of a prude". I find the short, short skirts and shorter tank tops on young girls much too revealing. Style conscious moms are spending more money on fewer clothes than ever before and these clothes are showing more of their child than necessary.

When I hear my grown son remark that these young girls are too scantily clothed I hear my own words coming out in yet another generation. When it is obvious to people his age, it is surely obvious to parents. The problem seems to be that no parent wants their child to be different; they want them to "fit" in with the crowd.

My Mother use to say, "Would you jump off a bridge if everyone else jumped?" I thought that was a silly question until I used it on my own children when they thought they should be allowed to do like others their age and I said "no".

Time becomes a blessing just as the agonies of letting children grow older are blessings. We stop and remember the looks on the faces of our own parents as we began our own new adventures in years past. Mom smiles, and I smile, and time slips away. Here I sit, seems like just yesterday, tears rolling down my face. He waves, I smile, he smiles, and time slips away.

Real Men Didn't Hug!

My father was a good man who spent time showing me how to change the oil in my old wreck of a car, how to change a flat tire and where the jack was located. Every time he worked on the family car I was underfoot ready and willing to help him even if he did not want it.

Daddy could fix anything, I thought. He could always come up with excuses why we did not need to spend money on frivolous items and we should save our wants for another day. His was a generation that rarely showed affection in the privacy of our home and would never ever do so in public. Only late in life did Daddy realize the value of a hug.

Like other fathers, he did not realize that saying the words, "I love you" was as important to him as it was to us children. Even though we never doubted his love, saying it and giving us a hug would have been an added "extra" for us and for him.

Leo Buscaglia, professor and lecturer on the subject of love says that most people do not hug because of the fear of being misinterpreted. Perhaps, because of men like him, whose hug ideas are for the purpose of improving relationships, we are beginning to notice attitude changes since he made this statement a few years ago.

As children we were taught that a hug could do many things. It can be a cure-all for pains especially when your best friend won't play with you. It is acceptance, affection, and a necessity for physical and emotional security for children. It is also a shame that in a few short years we have been forced to teach our children about good touch, bad touch experiences.

Many years ago I told the "man of the house" that he should hug our sons and not shake their hands no matter how big they got. Today our grown, 6 foot 3 plus sons know the value of a hug and are generous with them with their parents. We have sort of re-written the bumper sticker to read, "Have you hugged your parents today?"

Touch is a very valuable commodity these days. Advertising campaigns coax us to "reach out and touch" and hugs are prominent on political trails and public gatherings of every kind. The hug has become commonplace in our society and still we must caution our children about those who would use this to harm them or take advantage of their innocence.

In one generation we have moved from rare hugs for children to watch out for them. Surely something is wrong in our world when we progress so rapidly from security to caution in one act of kindness from an adult. Do we change the bumper sticker one more time to read, "Has anyone hugged your child today?"

Are we too big or too busy?

"The child hurries home from school excited about her day. Her parents will be home soon and she cannot wait to talk with them. Mother rushes in the door, arms full of groceries, and begins preparing dinner. The child starts to share her exciting day with her Mom who is very busy at the moment. "Not now honey, I will listen later." Dad comes home just in time for the news, and again the child begins her story. "When the news is over, sweetheart," he says. Later in the evening as the child is being tucked into bed, her Mom kisses her cheek and starts out of the room. "Mom," the child calls out, "Do you still love me even when you don't have time to listen?"

Shakespeare wrote: "we are like a poor player that struts and frets his hour upon the stage and then is heard no more." And another one, "full of sound and fury, signifying nothing." But what did the bard mean? Was he saying that many of us have limited time here on earth and worry too much about what we do and what we acquire that we leave the stage of life without making a significant difference? Did he mean that we talk a good game and express our needs to be heard and seen but what we have to say is of little consequence to others? Or did he mean that we squander our time on meaningless and selfish endeavors and fail to take advantage of the important?

It is the simplest of situations that seem to distract us from being happy or peaceful with our lives. We become caught up in the small and unimportant aspects of daily life and living and miss the small opportunities to make a person feel special. The wanting and desiring of material things gets in the way of our enjoying what we have already. For years we struggle to attain those measurements of success as prescribed by our peers or our social contacts, only to look back later in misery for misused moments of quality time that have been lost to us forever.

When we are young we are driven by a need we delegate to our upbringing, a wish for more than we had growing up. We compare our "stuff" with the stuff of others only to realize that the stuff we want also carries more responsibilities for care and maintenance. We want a better car, boat or house and the insurance and payments are higher. We want a better job, promotion, access to the elite people of our profession or community only to notice responsibility for actions and contributions of time and money go along with this progress.

We push aside the people we need and depend on for our happiness in a mad rush of time. We hamper and hinder relationships and obligations by our overwhelming need to be like "somebody else". Like the actor who struts across the stage to impress and be the envy of others, we see that the treasures we crave may one day be like the treasures of others, the clutter in booths of flea markets and antique store.

How do we make a difference? One possible way is not to give the appearance that we are in too big of a hurry to listen. Another is to take time to be a good friend, a good listener, and a good parent. Be willing to sacrifice some of our time in an effort to do something for other people. We all need to find time on our calendars to give portions of ourselves to make other people happy and we will be happy because we have found ways to express ourselves in unselfish acts of kindness and concern.

It isn't easy, putting others first. It isn't always convenient to listen to the long stories of children, but it can be an exciting adventure. It is not always an easy choice to fulfill obligations and put off personal chores of living, but this one thing I know, it is always worth the effort.

Go Fly a Kite!

The strong wind sent the porch rocker into a nosedive. The dog barked waking the "man of the house" from a deep sleep in his recliner. Jumping to his feet, the man of the house tripped scaring the dog and frightening me into believing a home invasion was in progress.

The Ides of March as Shakespeare called March winds, took over the home front this week and it was time to consider kite flying. I remember times in the past when the winds of March meant a trip to Fambro's Five and Ten or down to Jackson's Dime Store to pick out a kite suitable for high flying.

After two energetic boys finally decided on the appropriate kite, we would purchase a long ball of string and then head home to find light weight cloth to make colorful tails to help the kite fly.

As I recall, there was a great deal of running with the kite extended above the heads of the runners. The boy runners quickly tired and decided mom's arms would extend much higher and she would more than likely be able to get the kites airborne.

Needless to say, the enjoyment, after the endeavor to get the kites in the air was short lived. The rest of our time was spent retrieving them from trees and shrubs and patching a few holes which soon grew tiresome. I could never understand the dynamics of getting our kites in the air when less mature children nearby were shouting encouraging words about their high flyers solely for our less than perfect attempts.

It is in the moments of remembering when I realize just how much fun I had growing up with our children. How much they recall is still questionable even though they do remember the spill mom took in the creek. Building dams in the creek, riding perilously down the driveway on big wheels, scaring me half to death seems to be their favorite recalls.

I started on a mission to rid my closets of items that belonged to our grown children. I can tell you right away the process never took place. Instead I found myself caught up in "remember when" episodes. I looked at books, school papers, old tests and report cards and marveled at how fast time had passed.

I suppose the best advice I could give to hard working parents, and especially moms, is to be available for times to have fun. I am certain of this one thing: Children do not remember how much laundry you did but they will remember the fun you had with them.

As the wind whipped and churned the rockers, the dog barked and I recalled the kite flying days, I enjoyed thoroughly reliving the days of growing up with two wonderful boys.

Try Giving Yourself Away!

"Never before in the history of the world has the spirit of giving ourselves away been needed as it is today." These words are from a book entitled, "Try Giving Yourself Away," written by David Dunn in 1947. It has been reprinted twice since that date.

In 1977, my friend Bill Boulware, gave me a copy of the book and quite often over the last 25 years I have reread it with renewed enthusiasm. Of course, the biggest surprise is always the number of years I have had the book but I always recall the special friend who practiced giving himself away.

With a recent review of the book I became aware of the fact that in this day and time the spontaneous expressions of appreciation and good will are often looked upon with fear, and friendly gestures are accepted with hesitancy.

A child, perhaps five years old, was standing patiently with his mother while the clerk mixed paint for another customer. Once or twice he glanced up at me as I waited my turn with the clerk. I could see caution in his eyes as he glanced at me, and even though I consider myself to have a look of innocence, I was aware of his caution.

It was obvious the boy was interested in the machine the clerk used to add colors to make special paint orders. I spoke to the child and said the clerk had to add certain amounts of the various colors to get just the right one for his mom. He backed away from me as if he was frightened.

His mother smiled a s she said, "He has been told not to talk to strangers." How sad that we have come to the place where well meaning adults cannot share a bit of trivia with a youngster without the child being afraid. What a sad time we are in when a person like myself is trying to be friendly to a child with no ulterior motives other than just being nice and friendly.

Again I reread the helpful hints in my book. As I read the table of contents I questioned how small acts of giving ourselves away would be received today. Warmhearted impulses, the priceless gift of tolerance, little sparks of appreciation, noticing the extra efforts of others, being a credit giver, and neighborhood giving were some of the topics.

Everyday I have opportunities to speak to people, especially children. There are numerous times when I can say thank you, I appreciate your help, or you did a good job. I have found, however, that many people accept these acts of kindness and consideration with a somewhat hesitant attitude.

Perhaps, they see these gifts so seldom they cannot recognize nor appreciate them when they get them. Maybe they haven't practiced them in so long they have forgotten how to "give yourself away'.

In God We Trust

"In God we trust!" There, I've said it! It is on our
currency, in our Constitution, in our Pledge of Allegiance,
and engraved on public buildings. It does not disturb me
that it is not on every building or on every document that is
issued by the governments of the world. I am not appalled
that some people do not see eye to eye with me on all my
religious beliefs. Am I in the minority? Not at all!

Rabbi Marc Gellman wrote: "All religions teach us
to help people whenever we can. All religions teach us to
play fair and not to hit or steal or cheat. All religions teach
us we should be forgiving and cut people some slack when
they mess up, because someday we will mess up too. All
religions teach us to love our families, to respect our
parents and to make new families when we grow up.
Religions all over the world teach the same right way to
live."

In school we studied about western civilizations, the
crusades, wars, religions and the other major incidents of
history. We had our minds open to discover the many
interesting details of life in other nations. At least in my
time teachers believed all history was important.

In nations around the world there were many
religions. Many of these had 1000's of years of historical
facts and had artifacts preserved to verify their existence
for future generations. Some of these religions caused us to
wonder whether we could make the sacrifices expected of
their followers. Some were strict in their beliefs about
marriage, family, what to eat, and when to attend worship
services. We had a learning experience about them.

While every nation of the world may now recognize Christianity as a religion, it has not always been so. However, most people believe in something or someone even if that someone is an unknown entity who controls their salary better known as "the powers that be"...

Every state in the United States acknowledges God in their State Constitution. The national government has always recognized God's favor as needed in political documents. Even the Supreme Court, the highest court in our land, begins each session with the words: "God save the United States and this court."

How have we come to this point in history when we want to wipe away every indication that God has been an influence for right and wrong? What has brought about the fear that we may upset a few people by continuing to preserve the documents and heritage of 100's of years with the wording that is recognized as meaningful to our ancestors?

Even though all believers do not think alike this may be the time and place to say, "Enough is enough". Perhaps we should recognize that there is an important aspect to our heritage and preserve those artifacts of our country in their original state. Would that hurt anything?

The Heritage of the Young

In 1999, on a history documentary about the unrest and flag burning episodes during the Vietnam War, a poignant picture of a World War II veteran covered the screen. Tears flowed down his cheeks unashamedly as he watched young men set fire to the American flag. His face was etched with the horrors of his war experience and the dismay in the younger generation who did not seem to understand the meaning of the flag. The "rocket's red glare" for him had not been fireworks in the skies and the American flag was a symbol for the sacrifice of lives that were necessary to maintain our freedoms.

Young people have a way of challenging our society. A feature article in the Atlanta papers reported on teenagers who stated: "We will see X-rated movies one way or another if we want to see them!" One 15 year old child remarked that his parents would buy the ticket for him to go. Their reasoning was why keep them out of movies when they could see the same or worse on public television any day or night of the week for free. With a victorious look of satisfaction, they readily explained how they broke the rules of theater personnel.

Gun control, games of violence and killing, school bullying, taunting and harassing gangs, and moral decay are key words often used to describe youth. We hear a lot about how Johnny can't read, can't write, and the troubles he has in school. We are bombarded with information about test scores, more money needed for education, technology for every child, but it is also true that Johnny is having difficulty distinguishing right from wrong.

Add deep moral confusion to the list of educational problems. When young people know their parents will buy theater tickets to X-rated movies, allow them to purchase games of violence, and when adult leaders stand idly by as gangs terrorize neighborhoods, what does this teach youngsters? When money for education must buy metal detectors and security guards to protect our children in what should be one of the safest havens, their schools, what does this say about all of our values and morals?

Who is to blame for the moral indifference to patriotism, appreciation for our heritage and our freedoms as Americans? Where and when did we lose the standards of decency, honor, country, and respect for the lives and property of other people? Have we moved from a generation of Americans who cry at the burning of a flag, who were expected to be responsible for their behavior, to whom honesty was the rule and not the exception to a generation with measured indifference to moral, patriotic, and ethical traditions? Let us hope we have not!

Wrap it up in a neat package

Wrap it up in a neat little package: "Mark Barton killed innocent people because he lost his money in day trading the stock market." Wrap it up into a neat little package: "Bill Clinton's unfaithfulness to his marriage is because his grandmother and his mother fought over him as a child." Wrap it up in a neat little package: "Twin boys, age 11, kill father, wound mother and sister; we need gun control!"

Psychologists have a way of wrapping everything up into neat little packages that we can carry around with us from the time we are children until we are adults old enough to change our behavior. We have a tendency these days to grasp at straws of convenience to label and explain the uncontrolled behavior of individuals. We want to blame everyone but ourselves for our failures and take all the credit for our successes. But the neat packages are unfair answers for today's problems.

If a marriage gets complicated, wrap it up with a divorce. If a business or personal extravagances cause us to struggle to make ends meet, wrap it up in a bankruptcy. If our teenagers break their curfew or fail a subject, wrap it up with a threat to take their car keys or send them to their rooms with their video games and entertainment centers.

The modern day "out" or excuse for our behaviors are generally psychological and can be traced back to an insignificant incident in our childhood that relieves us of all responsibility. In other words, "Considering all my hurts, disappointments and traumas, I can't be responsible for the havoc I wreak in the lives of others or the mess I've made of my own! " Please forgive me if I don't accept that explanation!

What is it that makes us believe that only those people who have been graced with great genetics, perfect parentage and ideal social conditions can and will behave with character, courage and conscience? Which one of us can go through life without having obstacles, traumas, and troubles that threaten to strike us down? Who among us has lived a charmed life filled with happiness and no sadness, meaningful relationships with everyone we have encountered, and all the luxuries and none of the pains of this life?

There are many times in this life when our failures, guilts of things done or undone, and sorrows will lead us to despair and very low points emotionally. The worst part of crises situations seems to be that the person cannot imagine any other way out. They attempt with various means to run away from their problems by justifying alcoholism, drug addiction, violence, and yes, even love affairs as appropriate behavior.

Ardis Whitman wrote, "How do we learn to rise and walk; to cherish life against the exhaustion of guilt or sorrow or failure; to hold on until the lights come on again?" My answer would be to think of life as a neat package within itself! Just to have been born, just to have lived at all, how wonderful that is!

That is hard to believe.

I use this expression all the time: "That's hard to believe!" Watching the news and reading the local and Atlanta papers has made me use this expression many times and will probably cause me to use it many more unless I find an alternative phrase.

The awarding of $25 million in the O.J. Simpson saga of events was one of those times to express unbelief. I am one of those rare individuals who would like to believe he is not guilty but who is smart enough to know there is a wagon load of evidence against him. I am also guilty of thinking that Bill Clinton cannot be as bad as the media reports because the American people would not have been dumb enough to elected him President.

Corruption in the FBI, that's hard to believe! Corruption so bad that the evidence in the Oklahoma City and Olympic Village bombings may be tainted? Surely we have not allowed such incompetence to invade the highest source of law enforcement in the country.

And did you read the report about ebonics not being taught in public schools? It is hard to believe that educators would consider teaching yet another "language"(?) when the percentage is so high of students graduating from high school who cannot even write a correct sentence in English. It is hard for me to believe that the funding to teach children to speak English has been twisted and turned so many times that it now means students are taught in their native tongue to do math, science, and history.

We are still swinging that pendulum a long way when we are compromising our major language, English, and hiring seven translators for a citizenship ceremony because the people could not speak nor understand the language. Is the requirement still seven years of residency to become a citizen? If you have to spend seven years in America to become a citizen why not learn the language? Unbelievable!

Then we see the State Board of Education with a Time on Task proposal that will add five minutes to class time, reduce the number of days students can miss classes for field trips, deny course credit to students who do not attend classes, require a student to earn academic credits to graduate, and some people find these requirements hard to believe. What is hard to believe, you might ask! Well, since when was attending classes, receiving credit for courses, and instructional field trips, not a foregone conclusion.? The unbelievable was the change about the end-of-course test for Algebra 1 for 30% of the grade. What about tests for other courses?

It is hard to believe the changes in the thinking of mankind. How often have you used the algebra that you had to pass in high school and college? How many times a day do you find yourself in a business or professional situation that would require you to know ebonics? How many of you believe that O.J. will pay $25 million or will stop playing golf and making million on his "name"? Who believes that the FBI, CIA, or any other area of the Federal government is not in need of some house cleaning? If you answer "me" then that's hard to believe too!
*written 1997

Patriotism is Flag Concern

Over the Fourth of July, many people enjoy their annual run in the heated crowd of the Peachtree Road Race, while others brave the heat and hear the whistles of the steam engines as they experienced the gaiety of the Fourth. Some people remember the reason for the celebration as the fireworks filled the skies, and others hesitate once or twice to acknowledge the beauty and glory of the stars and stripes. Bodies are burned from too much sun and exhaustion overtakes revelers before the weekend ends. Many choose long, quiet, and restful weekends.

On a history documentary about the unrest and flag burning episodes during the Vietnam War, a poignant picture of a World War II veteran covered the screen. Tears flowed down his cheeks unashamedly as he watched young men set fire to the American flag. His face was etched with the horrors of his own war experience and also the dismay of how the younger generation did not understand the meaning of the flag. The "rocket's red glare" for him had not been fireworks in the skies and the American flag was a symbol for the sacrifice of lives, many of his friends, who sacrificed their lives in order to maintain their freedoms.

Young people have a way of challenging our society. A feature article in the Atlanta papers reported on teenagers who stated: "We will see X-rated movies one way or another if we want to see them!" One 15 year old child remarked that his parents would buy the ticket for him to go. Their reasoning was why keep them out of movies when they could see the same or worse on public television any day or night of the week for free. With a victorious look of satisfaction, these youngster readily explained how they always broke the rules of theater personnel.

Gun control, games of violence and killing, school bullying, taunting and harassing gangs, and moral decay are key words often used to describe today's youth. We hear a lot about how Johnny can't read, can't write, and the troubles he has in school. We are bombarded with information about test scores, more money needed for education, computers for every child, but is also true that Johnny is having difficulty distinguishing right from wrong.

We must add deep moral confusion to the list of educational problems. When young people know their parents will buy theater tickets to X-rated movies, allow them to purchase games of violence, and when adult leaders stand idly by as gangs terrorize neighborhoods, what does this teach youngsters? When money for education must buy metal detectors and security guards to protect our children in what should be one of the safest havens, their schools, what does this say about all of our values and morals?

Who is to blame for the moral indifference to patriotism, appreciation for our heritage and our freedoms as Americans? Where and when did we lose the standards of decency, honor, country, and respect for the lives and property of other people? Have we moved from the generation of Americans who cry at the burning of a flag, who were expected to be responsible for their behavior, to whom honesty was the rule and not the exception to a generation with measured indifference to moral, patriotic, and ethical traditions? Let us hope we have not!

Dog gone rascal!

Our family always had dogs. When I was in elementary school we had a dog named, Beaver. He was a red Chow and he was fierce in his protection of us children. Even though he never bit anyone, his growl discouraged people from harming us.

Later we had a black chow whose tongue was as black as his fur. He always rode in the back of my Dad's truck. He was lost in Canton one day and found his way home to Jasper some 25 miles away in two weeks. We believed the movies about dogs or cats finding their way home because we knew of several instances when our dog showed up at home weeks after being missing.

Needless to say, our young boys were very protective of a small dog who decided to make our house his home. The dog, appropriately named "Little" because we had a big dog, blessed us with several litters of puppies that were placed in good homes by the humane society. Each group of siblings cost much more than expected since we were giving them away.

This little mixed breed dog captured our hearts but when she got older her hearing and sight began to deteriorate. She lived her life as an outside dog and would only come into the house on very cold winter nights. Although she was not a big dog, her short legs carried her everywhere as the constant companion for two very active boys.

The man of the house has a best friend named Duke. He is a small white house dog and is appropriately named since the man of our house is a life-long John Wayne fan. Duke is certainly the master of our house and even though I held out against a house dog for years, he is ensconced as a member of the family now.

For weeks we were appalled at the news concerning Falcon player Michael Vick's involvement with dog fighting. His admission of his participation in the destroying of dogs that didn't perform was even more appalling. Several sportswriters have written that he needs to apologize. They think confession and repentance is necessary.

Atlanta Journal writer Jeff Schultz made the most sense to me. He wrote: "Michael Vick is not a great guy who made one bad decision. He is flawed. Not a little, but deeply." He continued: People of great character make bad decisions and rebound. They don't fund and operate illegal operations whose primary functions are to fight and kill dogs." Like this writer, I can't excuse Vick's behavior and decisions. It will take more than an apology.

Nothing Surprises Us

"Nothing surprises me anymore!" Do you find yourself using this expression often? When you read or hear an absurd story do you cringe from disbelief or do you simply shrug and let it zip through your mind and take up no space?

It seems we are living in a world of apathy and total disregard for morals, justice, and equality. Our leaders are lying, misrepresenting the truth, and avoiding justice and accountability through lawyers and counselors who alibi for them. Not only do we shrug about the President's misconduct but also we find ourselves "tired" of all this media hype. We alibi for him by saying we knew he was a man of low morals before he was elected and the Clinton joke of him living up to his side of the bargain goes in one ear and out the other.

We hear senators and representatives spouting their criticism and rhetoric from the rafters of the chambers of our nation's capital. A few days later these same holier than thou men elected to office because of their honesty and integrity, acknowledge that they had not kept an even greater oath of "forsaking all others", but that was 20 years ago, as if infidelity has a time limit.

We read accounts of couples that pick up hitchhikers for sex and before the evening is over the man is dead from his throat being slashed. We read or hear of teachers being killed, students killing other students, harassment of teachers by elementary school students and "nothing surprises us anymore". We discuss possibilities and guidelines of punishment or the purging of behavior problems from our schools and are told that students cannot be expelled from school more than 8 days out of 180, and why are we not surprised?

Men and women are teaching our younger generation that fighting and abuse are okay in the home. Parents are depriving children of a clean and healthy environment, and setting the example that behavior unbecoming is not only acceptable by them but that they will force officials to accept this behavior in schools and on buses. We observe the ridiculous outfits of boys and girls whose pants drag the floors and the pockets are below the knees. And no matter how ridiculous other generation's outfits were, the latest is an all time low. But nothing surprises us anymore!

We use to say with regularity, "can you believe that" and now we nonchalantly say "I'm not surprised." When we begin tolerating any and all behavior, whether right or wrong, we as a society are in real danger of moral decay. When we give approval by our silence and our lack of interest, then we will be condemned to an immoral and irrational society caught up in accepting no limitations and nothing will surprise us.

Our children cry out!

On April 20, 1999, Eric Harris and Dylan Klebold killed 14 students and one teacher. They wounded 23 others before killing themselves at Columbine High School in Littleton, Colorado.

We were amazed, frightened, and perplexed with the slaughter of children in our schools. We could not imagine how children could hate so much and could have such emptiness in their lives that death was preferable to life and the disregard for the lives of others meant nothing to them either.

The no tolerance, security sweeps, gun detectors, and bans on items that can inflict pain and death did not counteract yet another hate group. The Trench-coat Mafia group marched into their school, not as usual, but in an arrogant and destructive manner, killed their classmates, and then turned the guns on themselves. What horror and fear must surely have gripped the minds and hearts of parents and students in this Colorado town.

What has happened to the once tranquil, quiet, and safe atmosphere of our schools? Has the disregard for the law, the total emphasis on self, and the no consequence attitude of the 60's and 70's so manifested itself in today's young people that control is impossible and self destruction is the norm?

We asked if we had failed to instill in our young people the ability to discern good ideas from evil? Forget the fact that this is not the majority! The majority does not carry the guns and explosives, the majority does not killed, but numbers do count when there is death and destruction of our young. There were only two, but what immeasurable grief they caused by their actions.

We have moved into the future asking if we need to stop thinking in terms of allowing children to disrupt classes when the majority of students are there to learn. Do we need to stop giving alternatives to educating any child who cannot obey the rules and stop building special classrooms for "children" who ignore the rules of conduct and who disrespect teachers. Why should we "reward" them by placing them in a situation where other students can teach them alternative ways to avoid responsibility.

Many older adults have no tolerance for youngsters who are disrespectful, who bully their ways into the stores and malls, who use profanity with ease and yell out car windows at us. Many adults cringe at the sight of young girls wearing clothes that leave nothing to the imagination and we wonder at the intelligence of parents who are purchasing these outfits for their immature teenager girls. And we laugh at the big pants, the latest craze of boys who struggle with each step to pull up their pants so they can walk.

Our first response to the crisis situation at the Columbine High School was pain, followed by empathy for parents and students as they scrambled to reach each other in a terrifying situation. Next was disbelief as the numbers of dead and wounded increased. Then we reached the anger point.

There was an anger at the permissiveness of society to the improper behavior of young people, anger at a society that would not only condone but would allow destructive attitudes to flourish, and anger that adults could not halt behavior that was definitely contrary to school and society's standards.

How do we convince the "experts" to see the errors of their thinking? How do we, in good conscience, begin to take back the control of immature students and children in our schools, in our neighborhoods, and in our streets? How do we stop the violence? Can we begin by implanting into the minds of children a respect for the rights of other people, a respect for property, and a healthy attitude towards authority and the law. If we fail to get a grip on the situation, no place will be safe and we will continue to see other incidents of death and destruction.

* Virginia Tech Massacre occurred April 16, 2007. Thirty-two students and the gunman, Cho Seung-Hui were dead. Between 1999 and 2007 32 students and teachers were killed and 43 students injured in American schools shootings.

Media Madness

Do you ever have times when you have worked real hard to complete a job and no one notices? It isn't that you expected anyone to say thank you or that you had done a good job, but a mere acknowledgment of the task being completed would seem natural, but everyone is caught up in their own set of circumstances and the day passes without even a kind word or an expression of a job well done.

Do you ever have days when everything you say comes out wrong and is heard by ears that do not understand? Every word seems to be wrong no matter who you are talking with? Do you wonder how your foot keeps getting hung in your mouth and your words misinterpreted? Do you feel like you must have failed to pass verbal communication skills all through school and you need to start back to the time when you first learned to talk?

Have you ever had each and every event of your life probed and investigated? Has each opportunity of your life been shrouded with a black cloth of secrecy so that you do not even recognize them? Do you look around and every aspect of your existence seems to be falling apart and no amount of glue, tape, bandages or explanations can repair and heal the wounds?

If you have ever had one of these days, just think how President Clinton must have felt so many days of his life in the White House. He would come down for breakfast, turns on the news to find out who else had crawled out of the woodwork and was pointing an accusing finger at him. Hillary throws up her hands in utter astonishment and rushes to the phone to call their daughter to reassure her of their concern over the constant news coverage. And there was still a country to run, people to see, and pledges of support to be made by the man who spoke for America.

The President Clinton jokes, good and bad, were constantly circulating. The polls were updated daily to reveal the impact of the latest accusation of infidelity. The many deeds of indiscretion that he had been accused of doing seemed impossible in the reality of the demands of the office of the Presidency. Most of all, it was hard to believe that the position of President of the United States could be attained by a man whose moral standards were this absurd.

The book publishers had what we might call a "field day", and the lawyers, by the hundreds surface to speak for one person or another? And the women! Can you imagine wanting to have your name on the front page of every paper in the country saying a man, any man, had groped you and you didn't scream for help? Can you imagine the President having time to make a pass at every woman that came into his office? Indeed it is difficult to imagine any man who has achieved this degree of responsibility and credibility groping and insulting women.

There may be some truth to part of the accusations, but with so many out there now it will take years to determine which ones were true and which ones were false. My opinion was and is that he needed something to do if he had that much time on his hands. Maybe he did have too much time on his hands and should have taken up knitting or crocheting so he could keep his hands busy. You know the old saying: "idle hands are the devil's workshop!"

Are our priorities clear?

When Albert Schweitzer, the great missionary doctor, was a boy, a friend proposed that they go up in the hills to kill birds. Albert was reluctant, but afraid of being laughed at, he went along. They arrived at a tree in which a flock of birds was singing ; the boys put stones in their catapults. Then the church bells began to ring, mingling music with birdsong. For Albert, it was a voice from heaven. He shooed the birds away and went home. From that day on, reverence for life was more important to him than the fear of being laughed at. His priorities were clear.

The tragic loss of young people in a community touches the lives of many people and immediately, priorities are reconsidered and rearranged. Reports of accidents and the fear that another young life has been tragically erased, causes us to hesitate to look at the newspaper, but it also reminds us of the uncertainty of life itself.

We are reminded with each accident that death is a certainty and that the uncertainty concerning death is the when and where. We take our lives for granted and too often the miracle of living and breathing, happiness and even the despair of life are taken too lightly. We go from day to day planning careers, vacations, goals, apologies, or making major changes in our lives. We put off until a more convenient time the personal commitments we should make only to be rudely awaken to the fact that time is not within our control.

As parents or as children, we become so involved with our own jobs, our friends, economic struggles, fun or leisure time, that we fail to have even five meaningful minutes with each other. We neglect to call or write, we plan get-togethers that never seem to happen, and suddenly without forewarning those opportunities become "should have done's". We realize too late that good intentions were never adequate.

Too often we think that tomorrow is time enough to instill in our children an appreciation for life and family. We waste opportunities to teach them about drugs and alcohol, the dangers of inexperienced drivers in high speed automobiles, and the realities of injuries to the body and mind from poor judgment and wrong choices. Tomorrow will be soon enough to say we love them, to express our appreciation for all they mean to us and all they do to make our life happy, but the tragedies of late remind us that tomorrow may not come.

Are our priorities clear? Have we made the appropriate decisions about our own life and have we taken the opportunities to guide and direct others, especially young people to make the right choices for themselves? Have we overdone the freedom for young people as they silently cry out for more discipline? Have we put off until tomorrow those details of living that would prompt us to say, "I'm glad we had that time together!" Have our priorities been centered on ourselves or do we need to realign them? Ask yourself this question: "If tomorrow never comes, have I spent this day well?

Voltaire's Words in 1400 still true

In 1959 Allen Drury tried to capture the mood of
America when he wrote in his novel, Advise and Consent: "...the
legend crumbled, overnight the fall began, the heart went out of
it. Now there was a time of uneasiness...when all thinking men
fretted and worried about catching up and how to get ahead."

In the 1950's the days were hopeful and innocent but
many writers like Drury recorded them as anxious and
depressed. There was uneasiness among the young men and
women that made them seek the excitement of Woodstock and
the drugs, peace and free love of the Haight-Ashbury areas of
America. This feeling of unrest carried the tide of young people
into the 60's, 70's, and 80's, and the lust for drugs has not been
lost in the 90's.

The mood in America today is set by the media. The
writers, journalist, novelists, screenwriters, and the television
producers are providing us with the mood for our nation. In a
time of mass education we listen more to their ideas than we do
to the opinions of those individuals who would accurately point
out to us that in the long tape of history this period is only a few
short inches.

We are living in the times that certainly "try men's
souls". There is an ever-increasing crime rate, sex and violence
is accepted as the norm rather than the exception, and there are
drugs to relieve reality on too many street corners even in our
small town. The media reports this era as: unemployment is
down, a balance budget necessary, crime rates soar, corruption in
high and low places, and education and family values are
essential. There is no mention of the fact that families are
dysfunctional or lost in the shuffle of schedules, two incomes are
wanted but not always necessary, and day care is often
preferable to mothers providing the care.

The life style of people all over the world, not just in America, is better now than it has ever been. When you read fairy tales and see the illustrations of hunchbacks, hideous witches, and old hags with protruding teeth, you realize that people actually existed like that years ago. Now doctors can "make" you a face that isn't your own but someone else; your teeth can be straight and beautiful, and with proper adjustments here and there your body can be perfect "in your opinion".

But are people happier? We are cleaner, more attractive, more educated, more informed, more restless, and angrier than ever before in history. We have an avid desire to be the appropriate weight for our age and height, and to eat fat free and cholesterol free foods to keep us healthy and happy. We want more "stuff" in our possession, more pleasure, and more of the good life but fewer responsibilities.

We live in a world where we cannot be safe on the streets, day or night, safe in our homes, nor can we avoid the health problems and infectious diseases. Yet we must continue to believe that we live in the best of times. Writer Voltaire said in the 1400's: "Things may not be as they should be but they are as they are in this the best of all possible worlds." He could say the same today!

We were lucky, some are not!

David Pelzer's book "A Child Called It" had been on the New York Times bestseller list for five years and was given to me as a gift. It is the poignant story of the horrible physical and emotional abuse meted out to David by his mother from age 5 to age 11.

The headlines read: "Parents in Asia weep for a generation lost". Thousands and thousands of children were drowned from Indonesia to India by huge walls of water that decimated an entire generation of Asians. Can we even fathom the consequences of a generation of children lost?

Parents, family members, friends and strangers abuse thousands of children each year. However, the horrors of living day by day in a situation of fear are unbelievable to many of us. We think this does not happen in our community but alas, children still go to bed hungry each night. Children still are beaten and abused verbally and sexually every day of their lives in even the best communities.

Children have always been the helpless victims of cruelty, neglect, and abuse. Forced to steal food, sleep in the streets, try to survive in war torn countries including our own, children continue to be victims of adult decisions and mistakes. As we watch with apathy to the drawn and dirty faces of children in underprivileged countries of the world we are inclined to believe it does not happen here and now, but it does.

Children are our assets for a better world. They hold the keys to tomorrow and the
progress we will make in medicine, social and economic changes, and in food for nations of starving people.

Today's children are our links to the future and what we do for them now will make a difference in the next generation.

How are young parents handling discipline? How do they show love, and how do they respond to helpful instructions and guidance by teachers? Are we confused by the actions of parents who believe their child is perfect and fail to recognize places that "needs improvement."

We are all in this together as we wait and watch this generation of children. Will they be self-disciplined? Will they have good morals and ethics? Will they be adequate as leaders or will they succumb to bribery, deception, and deceit?

Are the examples we are setting for them good or bad? Are we willing to be involved to prevent abuse and cruelty? Are we doing what we should be doing when our children are watching? Are we being role models? When I read about abuse as in David Pelzer's case, I wonder why the neighbors did nothing to stop his torture. Are we not our brother's helper, especially innocent children?

Judge Nation said it all!

In March 2002 two young men vandalized an elementary school in Rockdale County, Georgia. The Judge sentenced the boys to serve nine years in prison, not just for the $200,000 in damages, but also for their inability to accept responsibility for their actions.

Judge Nation's words to these teenagers were the reason for my saving the clipping and are worth repeating. "I find myself in a difficult position. These defendants have offered age as an excuse. They have offered mental instability or illness as an excuse. They offered personality problems as an excuse. They offered drug problems and home problems as excuses."

This judge saw things differently. He accessed the situation as the community going too far to excuse the actions and to accept any behavior of young people. He wrote "You may sell this idea to somebody else. But not to me!"

We constantly ask the question, "What is normal in our society today?" Are we accepting of every type of behavior and excusing it on grounds of family, drugs, mental states, and personality problems? Surely we have not forgotten there are usually two sides to every situation, the right side and the wrong side. Have we begun to be so tolerant of improper behavior that we allow it to grow and grow?

We have become immune to the real hazards to our health. We get "up in arms" over second-hand smoke and ignore the stench and smoke from industries. We march and parade for the homeless people and fail to see the citizens living on small fixed income as being needy. We protest the war in Iraq and fail to wonder how our soldiers feel about our protests while they are defending our freedom to do so.

We all live in a difficult times when our own welfare is paramount to all other needs in a community. Churches and community groups do one-day projects and weekend "cures" for serious problems and believe enough has been done. Serious problems escalate daily and "band-aid" tactics are used to solve them.

We must begin making decisions that are sufficient to make a difference for the young people of tomorrow? We cannot continue to fool ourselves! We are a long way from making a difference.

10286016R00105

Made in the USA
Lexington, KY
25 September 2018